The Classical Monologue
Men

Michael Earley is a literary adviser and producer for BBC Radio Drama and Senior Editor-at-Large for Methuen Drama. Formerly Chairman of the Theater Studies Program at Yale University, he has also taught dramatic literature, acting and playwriting at the Juilliard School's Drama Center in New York City, New York University and various other places in the US and UK. He has worked in professional theatre as Literary Manager for the Acting Company (US) and Princeton's McCarter Theater Company (US).

Philippa Keil is a writer and translator who holds an MFA from the Yale School of Drama (US) where she acted, directed and studied dramaturgy. She also took an undergraduate degree at the University of Sussex, where she produced plays for the Frontdoor Theatre, and then worked professionally in London at the Orange Tree Theatre.

by the same authors

Solo! The Best Monologues of the 80s (Men and Women)
Soliloquy! The Shakespeare Monologues (Men and
Women)

The
Classical Monologue
Men

Edited with notes and commentaries by

MICHAEL EARLEY
& PHILIPPA KEIL

Methuen Drama

First published as a paperback original
in Great Britain in 1992 by Methuen Drama,
7/8 Kendrick Mews, London SW7 3HG

Copyright in the selections, format, introductions,
notes and commentaries and in the translated
extracts from: *Libation Bearers*; *Oedipus the King*;
Hippolytus; *The Miser*; *Woyzeck*; *The Government
Inspector*; *A Month in the Country*; *A Doll's House*;
Miss Julie; *The Seagull*; *The Dance of Death*;
The Cherry Orchard copyright © 1992
by Michael Earley and Philippa Keil.

A CIP catalogue record for this book
is available from the British Library
ISBN 0 413 66490 2

Printed and bound in Great Britain
by Cox & Wyman Ltd, Reading, Berkshire

Contents

French and Spanish

Restoration and Eighteenth-Century English

English and Irish (Nineteenth and Twentieth Century)

German, Scandinavian and Russian

Acknowledgements

Grateful acknowledgement is made for permission to reprint extracts from copyrighted material to the following:

Amber Lane Press for *Phedra* translation copyright © Robert David MacDonald 1985, 1991.

Harcourt Brace Jovanovich, Inc. for *The Misanthrope* translation copyright © Richard Wilbur 1954, 1955.

Methuen Drama for *Life is a Dream* translation copyright © Gwynne Edwards 1991, from *Calderón Plays: One*.

The Society of Authors on behalf of the Bernard Shaw Estate for *Man and Superman* and *Heartbreak House* by Bernard Shaw.

Caution

Notes to the Actor

A while back when we were putting together a selection of great monologues for men from Shakespeare's plays, appropriately called *Soliloquy!*, we knew that there would eventually be a need for a companion volume that would be an anthology of a limited selection of the great stage speeches from other ages of classical drama. This is that volume. It follows the course of drama from Aeschylus to Shaw, covering major periods and styles that also reflect the great ages of classical stage acting. In putting together this volume we have at last placed Shakespeare in an appropriate context. He is still in this volume but now as one writer among many glorious companions.

During the last decade there has been an unprecedented explosion of new productions of classical plays. The classical repertoire has returned with a vengeance as fierce as some of the monologues in this volume. More young actors and directors than ever before are exploring this rich vein of tradition, unearthing dramas which have languished on dusty shelves of libraries and showing them to have a size, weight and theatricality sorely missing in most contemporary work. The classical actor now stands on a par with the contemporary one. Learning how to be a classical actor is now every bit as important as knowing how to be a modern one.

Any actor, at some point in his career, must measure himself against the greatness of a classic text. All of these works have endured through time because they are filled with the very stuff that makes drama dramatic and theatre theatrical: tension, conflict, heroism, emotionalism, risk, danger and magnitude. This last item is particularly crucial, for in doing a classic piece of theatre an actor must instantly transform and enlarge himself mentally, physically and emotionally. The text gives you the capacity to do it. Once you surrender yourself to a great piece of classic theatre writing you really become a three-dimensional performer – the speech instantly showing each and every side of you. That is why these speeches are so terrific for auditions.

There is nothing timid or puny about the speeches in this volume. Any great classic speech is a gift for an actor and the last thing you need ever worry about is the fear of being inarticulate or boring. All the speeches you will encounter here have this one feature in common and in most instances they require you to pull out all the stops. You can wrap yourself in soaring lines of verse or prose as though language were a magnificent costume. They also require a strong voice and blatant physicality. You cannot hide behind these speeches but have to use them boldly to show off your skill and daring as a performer.

There are many ways of approaching these speeches as audition pieces, but the one thing you must do above everything else is approach them imaginatively. You must use the character's needs, desires, articulateness, spirit and wilfulness as a means of expansion. You must make imaginative leaps and substitutions so that you become the character himself caught in the turmoil of struggle. Few of the speeches here are naturalistic, most of them employ heightened rhetoric and none of them are stumbling or humbling. You must use the language like a trampoline that will launch you into acrobatic flight. On-stage, the best classical dramas give actors the capacity to soar; they enable the actor to be memorable by being moving. In the end your job is to move the audience.

The various commentaries and notes that accompany these monologues consciously avoid any instructions on 'how to act' these speeches. They are there to highlight interesting features in a monologue that you might not instantly see for yourself. They are also there to help you if you get stuck or confused about a particular speech or word. We have not written a series of 'director's notes' but really just appreciations of what is good about the writing from the point of view of acting. You the actor must make your own decisions about how, ultimately, to perform any of these classical monologues. There is not one right way to act these speeches. No two actors will ever do any of these monologues in quite the same way, which accounts for the thrill and unceasing wonder of live performance.

We would be foolish, however, not to admit that many of these pieces are a genuine test and challenge of your imaginative reach. So we have tried to include pieces of varying degrees of difficulty plus characters of different ages and experiences. The actor must bring to any of them an appetite for words and a willingness to experiment and play with infinite acting possibilities. Reading these speeches silently and understanding them intellectually will not help you very much to perform them. These speeches only reveal their potency and resonances once they are lifted off the page and taken onto the stage to be released out aloud. The solidity and power of great dramatic language live best when they echo in a theatre. Actors are the mediums of that release.

One last piece of crucial advice before you move on to the speeches themselves. No dramatic monologue can be satisfactorily detached and set adrift from its context within either a scene or the total play. Young actors especially, in a restless search for fresh audition material, will use isolated speeches without any familiarity of the plays from which they come. Acting does not work that way. You must see the character within the widest frame of reference – the play itself. You must read the play's full text in order to examine a character's complete needs and complex dramatic life. Before you can ever act any speech you must be certain why you, as the character, choose to say what you say now. The passion that all these speeches have in abundance requires your full engagement with the text. Acting in isolation from the total text is stilted acting, blind acting without insight.

Michael Earley
Philippa Keil
London 1991

A Word about the Translations

Except where indicated after specific texts, all translations in this volume are by the editors. At the end of the volume there is a 'Play Source' that points you to a published reading version of each script.

Libation Bearers (The Oresteia)
(*c*. 458 BC) Aeschylus

Mycenae. Before Agamemnon's palace.

*Orestes (18–20s) has been sent home by the god Apollo to avenge the
death of his father King Agamemnon at the hands of his mother,
Clytemnestra, and her lover Aegisthus. He does this with the aid of his
friend, Pylades. In this moment the palace doors are opened. The dead
bodies of Clytemnestra and Aegisthus are revealed, wrapped in the
same bloody cloth which they used to murder Agamemnon. Orestes
stands beside them and speaks to the Chorus.*

ORESTES.
   And so dies the tangled tyranny of Argos.
   They murdered my father, seized the kingdom's bounty,
   proudly usurped their thrones; now here they lie,
   lovers still, embraced in death.
   Double oaths were sworn: to kill my father,
   to love each other even to the grave.
   Both oaths are honoured.

   He points to the bloody cloth.

   Do you require evidence? Look, here it is:
   the trap they used to ensnare him.
   Look – here were his hands fettered, here his feet.
   Unwrap it, unwrap it. Gather around it.
   Do you see it, father? Not Agamemnon,
   but the bright Sun who is father to us all,
   who sees all that we mortals do. Do you see this,
   my mother's most unnatural crime?
   Apollo, god of the Sun,
   stand as my witness when this act is tried.

I killed her in the name of Justice.
But not him, not Aegisthus. His death was the callous
      Fate
deserved by every adulterer, condoned by every law.
Yet my mother's heart was nourished by hate
of the man whose children she bore in her womb:
her love yielding to hate, hate yielding to revulsion.
What name shall I give her? Adder? Viper?
Just touching, not even biting, poisons
and putrifies: Oh that monstrous, savage heart!

He picks up the cloth.

What name shall we give it? Give me a name,
an innocent name. A trap for a wild beast?
A shroud to wind round a dead man's limbs?
A web? A hanging gown to trip a man?
A ruse a robber might employ
to enmesh a traveller and wrest his wares?
A villain's contrivance! To murder people
And then to revel in the crime! . . .
She did it! She was guilty!
This is my proof, bloodied by Aegisthus' sword.
With the passage of time, death's discharge
has rotted all this gorgeous cloth.
O Father, now must I weep.
My hands hold this bolt of bloody cloth;
My heart howls for what is done
and what is to follow; a victory most hollow.

                                        [*lines 972–1017*]

COMMENTARY: The trilogy of tragedies that comprises Aeschylus' *Oresteia* (*Agamemnon, Libation Bearers, Eumenides*) dramatises the story of the return of King Agamemnon from the Trojan War and his death at the hands of his wife Clytemnestra and her lover Aegisthus; the revenge of her son Orestes who murders the adulterous couple; and Orestes' subsequent flight and trial. The doomed fate that hovers over the mythological House of Atreus is compounded by acts of regicide and matricide in the first two plays. Madness and fury propel the third play until a jury of Athenian citizens and the goddess Athena absolves Orestes of his guilt, ending the trilogy in concord. Like so many of Aeschylus' plays, the dialogue is written primarily as a series of lengthy monologues between a principal actor and the Chorus. The speeches are highly rhetorical and require an effectively sustained vocal stamina.

Orestes, like Shakespeare's Hamlet, is an avenger. As a prince he is reclaiming the throne that is justly his and not merely killing for the sake of vengeance. The killing of his mother is preceded by a harrowing scene between the two that is reminiscent of the Hamlet/Gertrude closet scene. The monologue is written like a defence plea: Orestes lays out the evidence for the jury-like Chorus – the corpses and the great royal gown – and proceeds to justify his actions. It is all done in bright sunlight for everyone (especially the audience) to see. Clytemnestra and Aegisthus are likened to tyrants and usurpers. It is important to realise that Orestes does not just see them as adulterous murderers but as political rebels who have unlawfully seized the throne. Orestes is both overwrought by emotion and filled with righteous rage. As in the great funeral oration of Mark Antony in Shakespeare's *Julius Caesar*, Orestes uses the event, and particularly the bloody royal gown, as a means of inciting passion in his listeners. This prop, coupled with the rhetoric, is crucial to the actor. Notice how rounded and open Orestes' words are, even though nothing in the English language can quite capture the sound quality of ancient Greek. After committing such a double killing, the actor can use the speech as Orestes' expiation for shock and horror which helps to motivate his indignation. The words are flung at the Chorus in princely rage and disdain. Orestes challenges them to interpret the act in the way he wants them to. His victory is marred by an anger that is still unsatisfied, and to prepare for his own flight and pursuit by the Furies, he must also admit that it is 'a victory most hollow'. So whatever satisfaction the slaying gives him, he ends the speech with a sense of foreboding and the actor must acknowledge this.

Oedipus the King
(*c.* 430 BC) Sophocles

Thebes. Before the palace of King Oedipus.

The city of Thebes is in the grip of a devastating plague. The oracle at Delphi has revealed that the murder of the late king, Laius, is the cause of the plague. King Oedipus (20s) places a curse on the murderer and swears to reveal him and so save the city. During the action of the drama Oedipus pursues various suspicions, one of which focuses on the facts of Laius' murder at a place where three roads cross. In this scene with his wife Jocasta, Laius' widow, Oedipus voices fears that he may be the murderer of Laius and recounts how he killed just such a man on the road to Thebes. His fear and forebodings cause him to make other connections as well.

OEDIPUS.
  I can keep it from you no longer.
  Wild forebodings fill my mind and urge me to speak.
  You have shared my fortune and have the right to know.
  Polybus, King of Corinth, was my father,
  and Merope, a Dorian, was my mother.
  I was acclaimed greatest of all men of Corinth,
  until one day something strange happened –
  something extraordinary – though not worth the distress
      it gave me then.
  At a feast, a man reeling with drink accused me
  in his drunkenness of being a bastard.
  I held back but inside felt fury and confusion.
  The next day I confronted my parents, my father and
      mother,
  repeating the accusation. They flew into a rage
  at the drunken fool and his lies.

Their reaction gave me comfort, but still it gnawed at
        me,
as the drunkard's rumour crept out and about.
Concealing it from my parents, I went to the oracle at
        Delphi.
The god gave me no answers to my questions.
But he did speak of other things, dreaded and horrible
        things:
that I would sleep with my own mother, and breed with
        her
an incestuous brood that no man could bear to behold.
And that I would be the murderer of my own father.
Hearing this I ran away, distancing myself from Corinth,
using the stars as my measure. Yes, I fled to a place
where I would never see fulfilled the dire evils foretold at
        Delphi.
And so my journey took me into that region
where you say King Laius was slain.
So Jocasta, now let me tell you the truth.
As I approached the place where three roads crossed,
I encountered a herald followed by a carriage with a man
        inside
just as you described it. He who led the horses,
and the old man inside, tried forcibly to push me off the
        road.
In outrage I struck the driver; the old man saw this and
waited for me to pass by him, and then he struck me with
        his
stick full on my head. But swiftly I paid him back plus
        more;
one quick blow from my staff sent him
reeling from his carriage down to the ground.
I killed him, and then I killed them all.
If this old man and Laius were bonded in blood
who could possibly be more miserable than I?

Who could be more hated by the gods; more reviled,
rejected and refused shelter by other men?
After all, I pronounced the curse on the murderer,
and the curse now falls on me! These very hands that
    killed him
have defiled you with their touch in his marriage bed.
Am I not evil? Corrupted and unclean? So I must be
    banished
and flee from Thebes. Yet not set foot in Corinth or see
    my own people
for fear that I might kill my father and marry my mother,
killing that same Polybus who begot and reared me.
Surely any man would be right to say of Oedipus
that all this is the cruel fate of the harsh gods.
Hear me, hear me you gods; by the purity of your power
over all human destiny may I never see that day come!
May I be swept from men's sight before I see
that deadly mark branded on me, sealing my doom.

[lines 771–834]

COMMENTARY: Sophocles' *Oedipus the King* is undoubtedly the most celebrated of classical Greek dramas. Structured like a good detective story, it sets out to discover a guilty man and bring health back to a city besieged by plague and the wrath of the gods. Through an unfolding pattern of evidence, Oedipus gradually recognises that he is the murderer who killed Laius, his true father, and is now married to Jocasta, his true mother. The tragedy of the play comes from this discovery and its impact: Jocasta hangs herself in shame while Oedipus plucks out his eyes and transforms himself into a pariah, exiled from the city of his birth.

Oedipus defines the questing nature of any actor: who am I and what am I? Throughout the play the actor is given pieces that fill in the overall puzzle of personality and self-identification. At crucial moments the character makes significant discoveries. This speech shows Oedipus peeling away the layers of the past in order to discover what really happened. Right away you can see what

6

the man is like: impulsive, proud, subject to rage and fits, blundering onto the path of truth as he becomes a participant in his own doom. Oedipus is not so much a tragic hero as he is a victim of fate. He comes into the world at the wrong place and the wrong time. As an infant, fortune and an oracle separated him from his natural parents, Laius and Jocasta; fortune then saved him from certain death in the guise of a kindly shepherd; and fortune then sent him to Corinth where he was adopted and raised by King Polybus as his own son. So Oedipus is a child of fortune who gradually learns the truth of his background and he is also an outcast who will stay an outcast. Throughout the speech the playwright creates a pattern of 'sight' and insight so that the actor can point the audience towards past, present and future significances. Oedipus literally sees his doom unfold before his very eyes. The truth is so overpowering that it blinds him in the end. The monologue is a long one in which tension is layered upon tension, and Oedipus ends it on the very crescendo of a discovery.

Hippolytus
(*c.* 428 BC) Euripides

Troezen (near Athens). In front of the palace of Theseus.

Hippolytus (17–19), son of King Theseus, has scorned sexual love and the worship of Aphrodite, the goddess of love, devoting himself to Artemis, the goddess of chastity and the hunt. In jealous revenge Aphrodite inflames an overwhelming passion for him in Phaedra, Hippolytus' stepmother. Driven to the limits of despair by her unrequited love, Phaedra hangs herself, leaving a suicide note accusing Hippolytus of having made an attempt upon her virtue. Theseus returns home from his travels to find Phaedra dead and believes the accusation in the letter, confronting Hippolytus in this scene. His son passionately defends himself, his honour and most of all his chastity.

HIPPOLYTUS.
Father, your eloquence and passion
sound convincing. You heighten your meaning
with a torrent of words, but separating sense from fury
your case is only weak and insubstantial.
I am not the kind of man who can sway a mob
with fine oratory. But in private company I can be
as eloquent as you. That is perfectly natural;
the boasting pretender who can persuade a crowd
with fiery words is justly scorned by learned critics.
Now necessity forces me to speak.
Let me reply to your first crushing accusation which
you believe is absolute and irrefutable.
You see these elements about you father – earth,
air and light – not one particle is more chaste than I,
though you would surely deny it. My golden rule
is to give honour to the gods first, and next to keep as
    friends

only men without sin, not men who profane
morality and indulge in evil. I do not mock my
     companions, father.
I am true to my friends whether they are in my company
     or not.
If there is one thing of which I am spotless, it is the very
     thing
of which you think you have condemned me.
To this day I am an absolute virgin.
Of the sexual act I know nothing from direct experience,
except what I have heard about or seen in images.
I have not done the deed. Nor do I desire to do it,
for my soul inspires obedient chastity.
If you doubt my confession of chastity,
then you must prove how your wife could have seduced
     me.
Was it because she was more beautiful than other
     women?
Or was I scheming to win her, and through her win
your fortune and your place as my prize?
Why, I must have been a complete fool, a dreaming
     madman!
Does being king have such appeal? Not for a wise man,
unless the corrupting allure of power has infatuated him,
and turned his head. I may desire victory in sport,
in the city I have no wish to compete at all,
but I am most content in the company of choice friends.
I am free to be myself; liberation from danger
provides a greater happiness than any crown.
I have still one last argument in my defence.
If I could call on one more character witness,
if *she* were still alive and present at my trial,
then facts would come to light revealing who was the
     guilty one.
As it stands, I can only swear to Zeus, the god of oaths
     above,

and to the firm earth beneath my feet, that I have never
    laid in sin
with your wife, nor desired or even thought of it.
Oh gods, if I have been such a guilty creature, then
may I die wretched and forgotten, a homeless and
    stateless beggar
in exile. May this earth and the sea refuse me refuge
    when I perish.
Whether it was fear that prompted her to take her own
    life, I can't say;
indeed, it is advisable for me to say no more.
In her act she showed honour, although she was not
    honourable;
I who live by honour now have it turned against me.

[*lines 983–1035*]

COMMENTARY: Euripides' *Hippolytus* focuses on the tragic hero
of the title. Other tragedies drawn from this same myth usually
focus on Phaedra. Hippolytus is central because he is tragically
caught between the rivalry of two goddesses, Aphrodite and
Artemis, and becomes a pawn and victim of their struggle. It is
not so much that Hippolytus rejects Aphrodite in favour of
Artemis, but that he makes such a cult of his virginity. He cuts
himself off from the very wellspring of life and for that he is
taught a mortal lesson. Phaedra is the instrument Aphrodite uses
to ensure Hippolytus' doom at the hands of his father.

Hippolytus is not an easy role to play. The character is young,
headstrong and defensive. He goes to such extremes to proclaim
his virtue and innocence that pride and arrogance threaten to
overwhelm his defence arguments. You can hear it in this speech
particularly. There is no remorse over the death of Phaedra, no
sense of impending danger. Self-righteousness and an abiding
faith in himself are some of Hippolytus' chief weaknesses. His
pronouncements and smug claims to being a 'virgin' are used as a
challenge to his father's more powerful rhetoric – a tool Euripides
gives the actor in this scene. Notice how Hippolytus catalogues
his virtues and cuts himself off totally from any kind of political

or civic engagement; the Greek citizens would have viewed this attitude as presumptuous. This is a very angry speech. Hippolytus uses it as a chance to vent frustrations which may have laid buried for some time. The actor should look at the entire scene from which this speech comes to appreciate how masterfully the dialogue between father and son is handled: it can still shock a modern audience. Graphic accusations are hurled back and forth as the rift between these two protagonists widens and deepens. The whole scene ends with Hippolytus' banishment. (See also Racine's *Phedra* on page 74.)

The Spanish Tragedy
(*c.* 1586) Thomas Kyd

Act 2, scene 5. Spain. Hieronimo's garden. Night.

Awakened by a scuffle in his garden, Hieronimo (40s–50s), a noble marshal of Spain, runs outside only to discover his son Horatio hanging dead from a tree in the arbour. Hieronimo has been an aloof and innocent bystander to all the political intrigues and machinations that have led to Horatio's murder. In this monologue he delivers an extended lament for the loss of his son.

HIERONIMO.
What outcries pluck me from my naked bed,
And chill my throbbing heart with trembling fear,
Which never danger yet could daunt before?
Who calls Hieronimo? Speak, here I am.
I did not slumber, therefore 'twas no dream.
No, no, it was some woman cried for help,
And here within this garden did she cry,
And in this garden must I rescue her. –
But stay, what murd'rous spectacle is this?
A man hanged up and all the murderers gone!
And in my bower, to lay the guilt on me!
This place was made for pleasure, not for death.

He cuts the body down.

Those garments that he wears I oft have seen –
Alas, it is Horatio, my sweet son!
O no, but he that whilom[1] was my son!
O was it thou that call'dst me from my bed?

[1] **whilom** formerly

O speak, if any spark of life remain!
I am thy father. Who hath slain my son?
What savage monster, not of human kind,
Hath here been glutted with thy harmless blood,
And left thy bloody corpse dishonoured here,
For me, amidst these dark and deathful shades,
To drown thee with an ocean of my tears?
O heavens, why made you night to cover sin?
By day this deed of darkness had not been.
O earth, why didst thou not in time devour
The vild² profaner of this sacred bower?
O poor Horatio, what hadst thou misdone,
To lose thy life ere life was new begun?
O wicked butcher, whatsoe'er thou wert,
How could thou strangle virtue and desert?
Ay me most wretched, that have lost my joy,
In losing my Horatio, my sweet boy!

[lines I–34]

COMMENTARY: Kyd's *The Spanish Tragedy* was one of the most popular and influential Elizabethan plays. It created a vogue for a ghoulish form of melodrama and its impact can be seen in other famous revenge tragedies, most notably Shakespeare's *Hamlet*. It is full of ghosts, deceit and outrageous villainy. The play also employs theatrically effective scenes and characters, calculated to excite an audience. An extremely political plot, involving the rivalry between Spain and Portugal, is thrown aside after Don Horatio, Hieronimo's son, is murdered by Don Balthazar, a violent Portuguese prince and rival for the hand of Bel-Imperia. The death and discovery of Horatio unleash a chain of incidents that culminates in the punishment of the villains and the separate suicides of Hieronimo and his wife Isabella.

Hieronimo's speech puts into words his emotional shock and horror at discovering his dead son. The brutal, macabre murder carried out at night in the garden creates a weird and forbidding

² **vild** vile

atmosphere which the character enhances with his speech as he verbalises a process of discovery step by step. He first reacts to the sounds he has heard outside, and then to what appears before his eyes. He even touches on the sense of speech when he tries to get his dead son to speak to him. The scene is alive to all the senses, and the actor can use these by picking up their pattern in the speech and physicalising them. The actor should also notice that Hieronimo expresses his horror in deeply vocalised vowels, particularly the 'o' sounds: 'O poor Hieronimo, what hadst thou misdone'. It is his way of experiencing grief and transforming it into words and laments. Sorrow becomes a deeply felt emotion echoed in the very words themselves. The blank verse lines, in many instances, are exclamations or questions and in playing you should give each line the full value it deserves. The scene is a highly dramatic tableau which presents a challenge for the actor who must perform with the corpse both as his prop, and also as a second character in the scene. It is best played when Hieronimo seems to expect the corpse to speak and answer the questions he asks it in the last third of the speech. By the final sentence he realises that he has lost his son forever.

Doctor Faustus
(*c.* 1589) Christopher Marlowe

Act 5, scene 2. Wittenberg. Faustus' study.

Faustus (40s), learned doctor of the University of Wittenberg, is the epitome of the Renaissance Man: skilled in all the liberal arts and sciences, ambitious, probing and full of pride and wonder at his own abilities. All this conceit naturally makes him ripe for a tragic fall. Having made a pact with the devil to sell his soul in exchange for twenty-four years of earthly power and delight, Faustus has reached his final hour and awaits his doom. The clock has just struck eleven as his speech begins.

FAUSTUS.
Ah Faustus,
Now hast thou but one bare hour to live,
And then thou must be damn'd perpetually.
Stand still, you ever-moving spheres of heaven,
That time may cease and midnight never come.
Fair nature's eye,[1] rise, rise again, and make
Perpetual day; or let this hour be but
A year, a month, a week, a natural day,
That Faustus may repent and save his soul.
O lente, lente, currite noctis equi![2]
The stars move still, time runs, the clock will strike.
The devil will come, and Faustus must be damn'd.
O I'll leap up to my God; who pulls me down?
See, see, where Christ's blood streams in the firmament.
One drop would save my soul, half a drop. Ah, my
         Christ.

[1] **Fair . . . eye** i.e. the sun
[2] **O . . . equi** O run slowly, slowly, horses of the night

Ah, rend not my heart for naming of my Christ;
Yet will I call on him. O spare me, Lucifer.
Where is it now? 'Tis gone: and see where God
Stretcheth out his arm and bends his ireful brows.
Mountains and hills, come, come, and fall on me,
And hide me from the heavy wrath of God.
No, no!
Then will I headlong run into the earth.
Earth, gape. O no, it will not harbour me.
You stars that reign'd at my nativity,
Whose influence hath allotted death and hell,
Now draw up Faustus like a foggy mist
Into the entrails of yon lab'ring cloud,
That when you vomit forth into the air
My limbs may issue from your smoky mouths,
So that my soul may but ascend to heaven.

The clock strikes.

Ah, half the hour is past, 'twill all be past anon.
O God,
If thou wilt not have mercy on my soul,
Yet for Christ's sake whose blood hath ransom'd me
Impose some end to my incessant pain:
Let Faustus live in hell a thousand years,
A hundred thousand, and at last be sav'd.
O, no end is limited[3] to damnèd souls.
Why wert thou not a creature wanting[4] soul?
Or why is this immortal that thou hast?
Ah, Pythagoras' *metempsychosis*,[5] were that true,
This soul should fly from me, and I be chang'd
Unto some brutish beast!
All beasts are happy, for when they die

[3] **limited** assigned
[4] **wanting** lacking
[5] **metempsychosis** the theory of transmigration of souls

Their souls are soon dissolv'd in elements,
But mine must live still to be plagu'd in hell.
Curs'd be the parents that engend'red me!
No, Faustus, curse thyself, curse Lucifer,
That hath depriv'd thee of the joys of heaven.

The clock strikes twelve.

It strikes, it strikes! Now, body, turn to air,
Or Lucifer will bear thee quick[6] to hell.

Thunder and lightning.

O soul, be chang'd into little water drops
And fall into the ocean, ne'er be found.

Enter the Devils.

My God, my God, look not so fierce on me.
Adders and serpents, let me breathe awhile.
Ugly hell, gape not! Come not, Lucifer.
I'll burn my books. Ah, Mephostophilis!

Exeunt with him.

[*lines 134–191*]

COMMENTARY: Marlowe's *The Tragical History of Doctor Faustus* follows twenty-four years of a life and is condensed into two hours of playing time. It is imbued with one of the great dramatic metaphors: the fall of man from the sin of pride. The play both looks back to the dramas of the Middle Ages and forward to the great Renaissance tragedies, even though Marlowe's text is quite uneven in quality. Faustus is a captivating but reckless character, flamboyant – like all of Marlowe's heroes – and exhibits only token remorse as the moment of his death approaches.

Time is wonderfully condensed for dramatic impact. This final speech begins on the hour, then the half hour and ends on the stroke of midnight. In between, Faustus makes a vain attempt to

[6] **quick** alive

hold back time. Notice how the language is full of cosmic visions; Faustus actually tries to straddle the void between heaven and earth, religion and intellect. The soliloquy is full of direct addresses to God, Christ and Lucifer, all of whom are personified as real beings, giving the actor very specific images to focus on. This aspect compensates for all the far-flung metaphysical rhetoric in the speech. The speech is enormously verbal and articulate; full of Latin phrases and delicious words like *metempsychosis*. The actor must remember that Faustus is the kind of character who feasts on words and ideas and goes to hell chorusing his own demise. For the most part the blank verse lines are end-stopped which means you can work your way through each one on a single breath. But do realise that as the speech reaches its climax, the power and import of the words swell along with the stage action. As Faustus runs out of time, the speech becomes more and more intense, breaking into small fragments.

Henry VI (Part 1) (1592)
William Shakespeare

Act 1, scene 5. France. A battlefield near Orleans.

Talbot (40s), a heroic English lord, leads his troops into battle against the French who are led by the fiery Joan la Pucelle (Joan of Arc). He has just fought Pucelle on the battlefield where the English are losing ground to the French. Talbot is fatigued and delirious from the battle and makes every effort to rouse his English troops to fight once more.

TALBOT.
My thoughts are whirlèd[1] like a potter's wheel;
I know not where I am or what I do.
A witch[2] by fear, not force, like Hannibal
Drives back our troops and conquers as she lists.[3]
So bees with smoke and doves with noisome[4] stench
Are from their hives and houses driven away.
They call us, for our fierceness, English dogs;
Now, like to whelps, we crying run away.

A short alarum.[5]

Hark, countrymen! Either renew the fight
Or tear the lions out of England's coat![6]
Renounce your soil;[7] give sheep in lions' stead.[8]

[1] **whirlèd** spun around
[2] **witch** i.e. Joan of Arc
[3] **lists** pleases
[4] **noisome** noxious
[5] **alarum** battle sound
[6] **lions . . . coat** the lion insignias embroidered on the English coat of arms
[7] **soil** native land
[8] **give . . . stead** display sheep in place of lions

Sheep run not half so treacherous[9] from the wolf,
Or horse or oxen from the leopard,
As you fly from your oft-subduèd slaves.

Alarum. Here another skirmish.

It will not be.[10] Retire into your trenches.
You all consented unto Salisbury's death,
For none would strike a stroke in his revenge.
Pucelle is entered into Orleans
In spite of us or aught that we could do.
O, would I were to die with Salisbury!
The shame hereof will make me hide my head.

Exit. Alarum. Retreat.

[*lines 19–39*]

COMMENTARY: Shakespeare's *Henry VI (Part 1)*, one of his earliest history plays, shifts focus between the English court and the French battlefields where the English are fighting to keep the territories conquered by Henry V. The play is full of quarrelling and political in-fighting among the English lords and the French aristocrats. There are also many bloody encounters on the battlefields of France where the French troops are inspired by Joan of Arc and the English by the heroic John Talbot. The events dramatised here plunge England into the civil strife of the Wars of the Roses which the second and third parts of the *Henry VI* plays explore and resolve. Although too infrequently performed, the play is filled with wonderful characters memorably sketched in small scenes and monologues.

John Talbot, a lord and later Earl of Shrewsbury, is one of Shakespeare's first great men of action. He anticipates later soldier-heroes like Bolingbroke (in *Richard II*), King Henry V and Coriolanus. He is forthright, professional and patriotic, unlike the other bickering English lords presented in the play. He seems to be fighting the French almost single-handedly. Because

[9] **treacherous** cowardly
[10] **It . . . be** i.e. it is hopeless

Shakespeare means to isolate one character to stand for an army, the actor must play Talbot with all the force of a battalion of troops surging forward and retreating. Notice that Talbot begins the speech in confusion and weariness (his head is whirling from the fatigue of battle). He has just encountered Joan of Arc, who is portrayed as a kind of witch, and he must overcome his delirium in order to marshal his troops to retreat. Notice how even in such a short monologue Shakespeare manages to evoke the full atmosphere and fierceness of battle. The actor must perform the speech above the 'alarums' and skirmishes of fighting and must be directing his troops with his words as well as having a private moment in the midst of a defeat. The lines are nicely balanced examples of blank verse and carry you right on through to the end; the words have a simplicity and directness so they can be heard above the noise on the battlefield (i.e. 'Or tear the lions out of England's coat' is the kind of iambic pentameter line that has a light/strong stress through each of the ten syllables). Talbot's fierceness is accentuated by the animal images he uses to express his contempt and frustration. This is a very concentrated, physical speech so use the emotional value of the vowels to demonstrate the strain of effort.

Arden of Feversham

(*c.* 1592) Anonymous

Act 3, scene 5. Arden's house at Feversham.

*Mosbie (20–30), the grasping and ambitious steward of Lord Clifford,
is carrying on an adulterous affair with Mistress Alice. Together they
have plotted the murder of her husband Thomas Arden, a wealthy
gentleman of Feversham in Kent, and have enlisted the aid of a motley
group of accomplices: the painter Clarke, Arden's tenant Greene and
Arden's servant Michael. As the action becomes heated, and several
attempts on Arden's life fail, Mosbie begins to suffer strain and guilt.
In this speech the effects of both begin to show and he discloses neurotic
fears about the whole enterprise.*

MOSBIE.
    Disturbèd thoughts drives me from company
    And dries my marrow with their watchfulness;
    Continual trouble of my moody brain
    Feebles my body by excess of drink,
    And nips me as the bitter north-east wind
    Doth check the tender blossoms in the spring.
    Well fares the man, howe'er his cates[1] do taste,
    That tables[2] not with foul suspicion;
    And he but pines amongst his delicates,
    Whose troubled mind is stuffed with discontent.
    My golden time was when I had no gold;
    Though then I wanted, yet I slept secure;
    My daily toil begat me night's repose,
    My night's repose made daylight fresh to me.
    But since I climbed the top-bough of the tree

[1] **cates** delicacies
[2] **tables** dines

And sought to build my nest among the clouds,
Each gentle stirry[3] gale doth shake my bed,
And makes me dread my downfall to the earth.
But whither doth contemplation carry me?
The way I seek to find, where pleasure dwells,
Is hedged behind me that I cannot back,
But needs must on, although to danger's gate.
Then, Arden, perish thou by that decree;
For Greene doth ear[4] the land and weed thee up
To make my harvest nothing but pure corn.
And for his pains I'll hive[5] him up a while,
And after smother him to have his wax:
Such bees as Greene must never live to sting.
Then is there Michael and the painter too,
Chief actors to Arden's overthrow;
Who when they shall see me sit in Arden's seat,
They will insult upon me for my meed,[6]
Or fright me by detecting of [7] his end.
I'll none of that, for I can cast a bone
To make these curs pluck out each other's throat,[8]
And then am I sole ruler of mine own.
Yet Mistress Arden lives; but she's myself,
And holy Church rites makes us two but one.
But what for that? I may not trust you, Alice:
You have supplanted Arden for my sake,
And will extirpen[9] me to plant another.
'Tis fearful sleeping in a serpent's bed,
And I will cleanly rid my hands of her.

---

[3] **stirry** moving, eventful
[4] **ear** plough (Greene has been sent to carry out the actual murder.)
[5] **hive** contain him, as in a beehive
[6] **insult . . . meed** cast aspersions on my gain
[7] **detecting of** revealing
[8] **cast . . . throat** set the dogs one against the other
[9] **extirpen** exterminate

Enter Alice.

But here she comes, and I must flatter her.

[*lines 1–45*]

COMMENTARY: *Arden of Feversham* is a domestic tragedy and probably the first and best example of this genre in Elizabethan drama. Rather than deal with royalty it deals with a middle-class family. The action of the play centres on the efforts of Mistress Alice Arden and her lover Mosbie to plot and execute the murder of Alice's husband, Thomas Arden. The play is full of sensational twists and turns of plot, events both highly dramatic and melodramatic that threaten to turn it into farce at some points. The play was based on a notorious murder committed in 1551 and presages Shakespeare's *Macbeth*. In a recent revival of the play it was clearly shown that the roles are as lively and actable today as they would have been in the sixteenth century. Since the motivations of the characters come from real human needs rather than from metaphysical ones, everything they say and do has a reason and cause.

Mosbie has been off-stage for several scenes. During that time guilt has begun to prey on him. He enters to deliver this soliloquy at a heightened and fevered pitch. Driven to distraction – and drink – Mosbie shares with the audience the effects of his murderous intents and his fears for himself; they literally chill him to the bone. The psychological pressure is beginning to make Mosbie crack just as it does Macbeth at the same point in Shakespeare's play. He reflects on a past when he was not racked by guilt: 'My golden time was when I had no gold; / Though then I wanted, yet I slept secure.' You can hear in the speech that Mosbie (again like Macbeth) is suffering from lack of sleep. A good part of the speech, too, is about his growing suspicion of his co-conspirators. Mosbie realises he can trust no one, least of all Alice: he suspects that he could eventually become her next victim when they are married. From an acting point of view this whole monologue is a build-up for the confrontation scene that directly follows between Alice and Mosbie after the end of this speech. The blank verse lines are simply constructed and practically all end-stopped as complete thoughts. Move through the speech line by line, picking up emotions as they accumulate.

Edward II
(*c.* 1594) Christopher Marlowe

Act 1, scene 1. London. A street.

This is the opening moment of the play and Gaveston (20s) enters reading a letter. Piers de Gaveston, a Gascon courtier and afterwards made Earl of Cornwall, is a favourite of King Edward II. He was banished from the realm by Edward's father and is summoned back to England by the young and newly crowned king. Here Gaveston muses on what influence he will have over the monarch.

GAVESTON (*reading a letter that was brought him from the King*).
    'My father is deceas'd, come Gaveston,
    And share the kingdom with thy dearest friend.'
    Ah, words that make me surfeit with delight!
    What greater bliss can hap[1] to Gaveston
    Than live and be the favourite of a king?
    Sweet prince I come; these, these, thy amorous lines
    Might have enforc'd me to have swum from France,
    And like Leander[2] gasp'd upon the sand,
    So thou wouldst smile and take me in thy arms.
    The sight of London to my exil'd eyes
    Is as Elysium[3] to a new-come soul.
    Not that I love the city or the men,
    But that it harbours him I hold so dear,
    The king, upon whose bosom let me die,[4]
    And with the world be still at enmity.

[1] **hap** bestow fortune upon
[2] **Leander** a legendary Greek youth who swam the Hellespont nightly to visit Hero
[3] **Elysium** i.e. Paradise
[4] **let me die** i.e. swoon

What need the arctic people love star-light
To whom the sun shines both by day and night?
Farewell base stooping to the lordly peers;
My knee shall bow to none but to the king.
As for the multitude, that are but sparks
Rak'd up in embers of their poverty,
Tanti![5] I'll fawn[6] first on the wind,
That glanceth at my lips and flieth away.
But how now what are these.

Enter three poor men.

[*lines 1–25*]

COMMENTARY: Marlowe's *Edward II* is a good example of a chronicle or history play that charts the changing fortunes and fall of a monarch. Characters are thrust into power and then have it snatched away as the constant turning of Fortune's Wheel drives the dramatic action towards a deadly conclusion. During the reign of Edward I, Piers Gaveston, favourite of the Prince of Wales, was banished from the realm. He hurries back to London from France upon receiving the sudden news that the old king is dead and that he has been invited to share in the kingdom with his dear friend, now King Edward II. The relationship between these two characters, frequently portrayed as a homoerotic love affair, produces only jealousy and anger among the peers of the realm. They first plot Gaveston's downfall and then Edward's hideous death.

This speech, which opens the play, begins with Gaveston reading the letter from Edward and delighting in his sudden reversal of fortune. He cannot contain his joy so he must speak it out loud. Gaveston is openly portrayed by Marlowe as an outsider and a blatant opportunist. It is never clear if he loves Edward with the same intensity and sincerity as the young king does him. His return to London from France ignites a cycle of tragic events which his monologue unwittingly portends: Leander who swam the Hellespont to his lover Hero eventually died in one of his

[5] **Tanti!** So much for them
[6] **fawn** cringe

26

attempts. So although Gaveston is full of hope and ambition we know right from the start that pride makes him ready for a fall. When an actor speaks Gaveston's lines he suddenly finds himself in the company of a supreme egoist who speaks extravagantly. This is really the speech of an eager lover – the word 'amorous' is a tip-off – and Edward treats Gaveston as exactly that in front of the whole court. Gaveston uses wonderful images and classical allusions to describe his fortunate situation. He is a sensualist as far as words are concerned. 'Ah, words that make me surfeit with delight!' is one of his typical iambic pentameter lines; words have the quality of food and are fed upon. The physical images of swimming, gasping and embracing enlarge the capacity of the speech beyond the merely verbal. As Gaveston relishes his fortunate circumstances he literally transforms himself through words.

Edward II
(*c.* 1594) Christopher Marlowe

Act 5, scene 1. A room in Kenilworth Castle.

Edward II (20s) has been an impulsive and irresponsible monarch foolishly ignoring the growing power of certain peers in his realm. Their rebellion against his rule has led to his overthrow. In this scene he surrenders his crown to the Earl of Leicester and the Bishop of Winchester, but does so unwillingly.

EDWARD.
    Ah, Leicester, weigh how hardly I can brook[1]
    To lose my crown and kingdom without cause,
    To give ambitious Mortimer my right,
    That like a mountain overwhelms my bliss;
    In which extreme my mind here murdered is.
    But what the heavens appoint, I must obey.
    Here, take my crown, the life of Edward too.

He takes off the crown.

    Two kings in England cannot reign at once.
    But stay awhile, let me be king till night,
    That I may gaze upon this glittering crown;
    So shall my eyes receive their last content,
    My head the latest honour due to it,
    And jointly both yield up their wishèd right.
    Continue ever, thou celestial sun,
    Let never silent night possess this clime;
    Stand still, you watches of the element,[2]
    All times and season rest you at a stay,

[1] **brook** tolerate
[2] **element** sky

That Edward may be still fair England's king!
But day's bright beams doth vanish fast away,
And needs I must resign my wishèd crown.
Inhuman creatures, nurs'd with tiger's milk,
Why gape you for your sovereign's overthrow –
My diadem, I mean, and guiltless life?
See, monsters, see, I'll wear my crown again!

He puts on the crown.

What, fear you not the fury of your king?
But hapless Edward, thou art fondly[3] led;
They pass not for thy frowns as late they did,
But seek to make a new elected king;
Which fills my mind with strange despairing thoughts;
Which thoughts are martyred with endless torments;
And in this torment, comfort find I none,
But that I feel the crown upon my head.
And therefore let me wear it yet awhile

[*lines 51–83*]

COMMENTARY: During the up-and-down struggle for power which constitutes the main action of Marlowe's *Edward II*, the king's peers, chief among them Roger Mortimer, plot to seize his crown. After Edward has been captured at Kenilworth Castle he is forced to abdicate in favour of his son and is sent to his imprisonment. Edward's weakness as a ruler and his obsession with his friend Piers de Gaveston (*see previous speech*) have been two of the chief causes of his downfall. In the eyes of his nobles and his church he is an unfit ruler. Not even his divine right to the crown can save him at this point.

This abdication scene, like a similar scene in Shakespeare's *Richard II*, focuses on the symbolic and actual surrendering of a crown. The actor is working with a prop which symbolises Edward's divine right to rule. At one point in the speech Edward

[3] **fondly** foolishly

puts the crown on his head expecting it to give him instant power and authority. The crown has an aura and cannot be handled too lightly. Edward endows the crown with great reverence and value; look at how many different ways he refers to it. Central to the speech is Edward's sudden unwillingness to part with the crown and the role it symbolises. He just cannot give it up. Even though he has a capricious nature, when it comes to a dramatic moment like this his kingliness suddenly asserts itself and he grows in stature. Notice how he tries to hold back and stop time in the speech: 'Stand still, you watches of the element, / All times and season rest you at a stay.' If done well this can be a highly dramatic manoeuvre as Edward ekes out the moments in small drops, almost as if he is restraining a full flood of emotions. Notice how many of the blank verse lines are end-stopped. You can comfortably take each one as a separate thought and endow it with significance. The iambic pentameter is also quite regular and pounds out a steady rhythm to evoke Edward's authority. In the life of a king no moment could be more tragic and harrowing than the surrender of a crown. His life and the crown are fatally intertwined.

Romeo and Juliet
(*c.* 1595) William Shakespeare

Act 5, scene 1. Mantua. A street.

Romeo (18–20s) is in exile from Verona for the killing of Tybalt in a street fight. In the first speech he reports on a dream he has had of Juliet which has put him in a cheerful mood. In the second speech, however (a bit further along in the scene), his manservant Balthasar, newly arrived from Verona with sad news, reports that Juliet is dead and lying in her family tomb. Romeo, wild with fear and panic, resolves to return to Verona despite everything and join Juliet in death. He decides to commit suicide and will seek the means of doing so from a nearby apothecary shop.

ROMEO.
    If I may trust the flattering[1] truth of sleep,
    My dreams presage[2] some joyful news at hand.
    My bosom's lord[3] sits lightly in his throne,[4]
    And all this day an unaccustomed spirit
    Lifts me above the ground with cheerful thoughts.
    I dreamt my lady came and found me dead –
    Strange dream that gives a dead man leave to think! –
    And breathed such life with kisses in my lips,
    That I revived, and was an emperor.
    Ah me, how sweet is love itself possessed,[5]
    When but love's shadows[6] are so rich in joy.

---

[1] **flattering** encouraging and pleasurable
[2] **presage** foretell
[3] **bosom's lord** Cupid (i.e. love)
[4] **throne** i.e. heart
[5] **itself possessed** actually enjoyed
[6] **shadows** dreams, fancies

Enter Balthasar his man, booted.

News from Verona! How now Balthasar,
Dost thou not bring me letters from the friar?
How doth my lady? Is my father well?
How fares my Juliet? That I ask again,
For nothing can be ill if she be well.

[*lines 1–16*]

Well, Juliet, I will lie with thee tonight.
Let's see for means.[7] O mischief[8] thou art swift
To enter in the thoughts of desperate men.
I do remember an apothecary[9] –
And hereabouts 'a dwells – which late I noted,[10]
In tattered weeds,[11] with overwhelming brows,[12]
Culling of simples.[13] Meagre[14] were his looks,
Sharp misery had worn him to the bones;
And in his needy[15] shop a tortoise hung,
An alligator stuffed, and other skins
Of ill-shaped fishes; and about his shelves
A beggarly account[16] of empty boxes,
Green earthen pots, bladders, and musty seeds,
Remnants of packthread,[17] and old cakes of roses,[18]
Were thinly scattered, to make up a show.
Noting this penury, to myself I said,
'An if a man did need a poison now,

---

[7] **for means** by what means
[8] **mischief** misfortune, calamity
[9] **apothecary** druggist
[10] **late I noted** recently noticed
[11] **weeds** garments
[12] **overwhelming brows** prominent eyebrows
[13] **Culling of simples** gathering medicinal herbs
[14] **Meagre** impoverished
[15] **needy** poor
[16] **beggarly account** wretched collection
[17] **packthread** twine
[18] **cakes of roses** compressed rose petals for perfume

Whose sale is present death in Mantua,[19]
Here lives a caitiff [20] wretch would sell it him.'
O this same thought did but forerun[21] my need,
And this same needy man must sell it me.
As I remember, this should be the house.
Being holiday, the beggar's shop is shut.
What ho, apothecary!

[*lines 34–57*]

COMMENTARY: Shakespeare's *Romeo and Juliet* explores the tragic plight of two young lovers whose families, the Montagues and Capulets, are feuding enemies in Verona. The blossoming love between Romeo and Juliet is suddenly destroyed when Romeo kills Juliet's kinsman Tybalt in a sword fight. As a punishment Romeo is exiled to Mantua. With the aid of Friar Laurence, Juliet thwarts her parents' plans to marry her to Paris by feigning death by means of a sleeping potion. But Romeo, ignorant of this plan, receives the wrong signals. Thinking she is really dead, he rushes back to Verona and commits suicide by her sleeping body. When she awakens she too kills herself in despair with Romeo's dagger. The tragic ending ironically joins the two houses in mutual mourning, finally healing their ancient feud.

In these contrasting speeches Romeo shows two of the emotional poles that the actor in this play must swing between. In the first speech his enjoyable dream has energised his spirits and the language he uses is romantically uplifting. Notice the long/soft vowel/consonant sounds he combines: 'presage', 'bosom', 'ground', 'dream', 'kisses', 'lips', 'sweet', 'love', 'joy'. The speech carries Romeo back to the sweet dreaminess of the balcony scene (Act 2, scene 2). When Balthasar enters, having just travelled back from Verona, Romeo overwhelms him with questions. The actor can either do this quickly, leaving Balthasar no room to reply, or wait for replies which never come because the news is so dire, using each question to try and get a response. In the second

[19] **Whose . . . Mantua** i.e. the illegal sale of which would be punished by death in Mantua
[20] **caitiff** despicable
[21] **forerun** precede

speech, after Balthasar's report, the mood has darkened. Romeo now believes Juliet is dead. Romance turns to desperation. The wretched apothecary's shop becomes the image and stimulus for his suicide plan and the actor can use details from the image to feed his dejection. The language has a deathly pall to it: the vowel/consonant sounds have now lowered in tone and have an ominous ring: 'green earthen pots, bladders and musty seeds', etc. A world of delight has become dark and morbid.

Hamlet
(1601) William Shakespeare

Act 5, scene 1. Elsinore. A churchyard.

Hamlet (20s) has recently returned to Denmark from exile. Together with his friend Horatio he comes into a graveyard near the castle at Elsinore and encounters two gravediggers at work. Hamlet engages in comic repartee with the first gravedigger who shows him a skull. It is that of Yorick, the former jester at the court of Hamlet's late father. Taking the skull, Hamlet muses on its significance.

HAMLET.
Let me see. (*He takes the skull.*) Alas, poor Yorick! I knew him, Horatio, a fellow of infinite jest, of most excellent fancy. He hath bore me on his back a thousand times, and now how abhorred in my imagination it is! My gorge[1] rises at it. Here hung those lips that I have kissed I know not how oft. Where be your gibes[2] now? Your gambols,[3] your songs, your flashes of merriment that were wont to set the table on a roar? Not one now, to mock your own grinning?[4] Quite chopfallen?[5] Now get you to my lady's chamber and tell her, let her paint[6] an inch thick, to this favour she must come.[7] Make her laugh at that. Prithee, Horatio, tell me one thing . . . Dost thou think Alexander looked o' this fashion i' th' earth? . . . And smelt so? Pah! (*He puts down the skull.*) . . . To what base uses we may return, Horatio!

[1] **gorge** vomit
[2] **gibes** taunts
[3] **gambols** playful cavorting
[4] **mock . . . grinning** i.e. laugh at the comic faces you make
[5] **chopfallen** (1) downcast (2) lacking a lower jaw
[6] **paint** put on her make-up
[7] **to . . . come** i.e. she must do this to her face

Why may not imagination trace the noble dust of Alexander till 'a find it stopping a bunghole?[8]

[HORATIO. 'Twere to consider too curiously to consider so.]

No, faith, not a jot, but to follow him thither with modesty[9] enough, and likelihood to lead it. As thus: Alexander died, Alexander was buried, Alexander returneth to dust, the dust is earth, of earth we make loam,[10] and why of that loam whereto he was converted might they not stop a beer barrel?
Imperious Caesar, dead and turned to clay,
Might stop a hole to keep the wind away.
O, that that earth which kept the world in awe
Should patch a wall t'expel the winter's flaw![11]

COMMENTARY: Shakespeare's *Hamlet* is a tragedy wide in its reach. The title role is also the greatest in the classical repertoire, providing some of the most memorable soliloquies in drama. In its most basic form it is a revenge play that pits Prince Hamlet against his devious uncle Claudius who has murdered Hamlet's father and married his mother Queen Gertrude. The ramifications of this fratricide and swift marriage have thrown Denmark into turmoil along with the prince himself. Hamlet's delay and subsequent decision to take revenge by killing Claudius form the main action of the play, but it also takes numerous digressions into other areas that comment on the main action and allow Hamlet to expound on various philosophical notions governing existence. The climactic duel scene kills all the main protagonists and antagonists ending the play on a sombre, moody note.

By this point in the final act, Hamlet has returned to Denmark a changed man. He does not yet know that his love, Ophelia, has

[8] **bunghole** hole in a barrel for pouring liquid through
[9] **modesty** restraint
[10] **loam** a mix of clay and water, used in making bricks, plastering, etc.
[11] **flaw** sudden gust of wind

committed suicide and that the grave he is standing by is being prepared to receive her body. Before his exile, he was feigning madness and actually seemed mad, finding it hard to kill Claudius even though he had proof in hand. The delay occupied the first four acts of the play. The final act moves swiftly and Hamlet displays a new resolve. In this speech, for instance, notice how calm, simple and even playful Hamlet is in the face of death. Death's face, in fact, is that of a jester and the skull is a blackly humorous prop for the actor to use in this scene. It is a very informal scene written in prose, except for the rhyming quatrain at the end (a piece of comic doggerel). The speech also covers time, reaching back in the past to Alexander the Great and the actor must speak the speech simply, but also sound its deeper, graver resonances. Words like 'poor Yorick', 'abhorred', 'gorge', 'bore', 'chopfallen', 'earth', 'buried' give you a sense of the depth that the speech contains. They also tell you that the speech cannot be rushed; give time for Hamlet's ruminations to develop. The actor has to convey the hard fact that all of us will return in the end to dust. Do not miss, however, any chance you see for ironic humour. It is in Hamlet's nature to be both severe and frivolous simultaneously.

A Woman Killed with Kindness
(1603) Thomas Heywood

Scene 6. Yorkshire. A room in the home of Master John Frankford.

Wendoll (20s–30s), a gentleman, contemplates seducing the faithful wife of his friend and host, Master John Frankford. In this speech Wendoll reveals his desires and obsessions.

WENDOLL.
   I am a villain, if I apprehend[1]
   But such a thought! Then, to attempt the deed,
   Slave, thou art damned without redemption. –
   I'll drive away this passion with a song.
   A song! Ha, ha! A song! As if, fond[2] man,
   Thy eyes could swim in laughter, when thy soul
   Lies drenched and drowned in red tears of blood!
   I'll pray, and see if God within my heart
   Plant better thoughts. Why, prayers are meditations,
   And when I meditate (oh, God forgive me!)
   It is on her divine perfections.
   I will forget her; I will arm myself
   Not t'entertain a thought of love to her;
   And, when I come by chance into her presence,
   I'll hale these balls,[3] until my eye-strings crack
   From being pulled and drawn to look that way.

Enter, over the Stage, Frankford, his wife, and Nicholas and exeunt.

   O God, O God! With what a violence
   I'm hurried to mine own destruction!

[1] **apprehend** even imagine
[2] **fond** foolish
[3] **hale . . . balls** i.e. constrain my glances at her

38

There goest thou, the most perfectest man
That ever England bred a gentleman,
And shall I wrong his bed? – Thou God of thunder!
Stay, in Thy thoughts of vengeance and of wrath,
Thy great, almighty, and all-judging hand
From speedy execution on a villain, –
A villain and a traitor to his friend.   [*lines 1–25*]

COMMENTARY: The main plot of Thomas Heywood's domestic tragedy *A Woman Killed with Kindness* revolves around the duplicity of Wendoll towards his friend John Frankford ('the most perfectest man / That ever England bred a gentleman') and the eventual adultery between Wendoll and Frankford's wife Anne. Gradually Frankford accepts the evidence of his wife's and friend's infidelity and punishes her not by branding her an adulteress but by tormenting her with kindness and exiling her from his sight. She eventually dies by pining away and Wendoll flees the scene.

Wendoll immediately identifies what he thinks he is – a villain. His treachery is compounded by the fact that he betrays the trust of his host, though adultery is the greatest of the sins he commits. In this speech he attempts to drive away his guilty thoughts in song – this is a bold bit of acting which is difficult to bring off without. seeming too comic – and then he resorts to prayer. Wendoll is in the grips of an obsessive despair which drives him to speak in a stream of consciousness. The mid-line breaks in the verse divide each thought into small units which helps make them sound more naturalistic when spoken. Words, in the form of self-castigation, tumble out of him. The speech is full of antithesis (one side of himself battling with the other; good versus evil). Just when he has resolved never to look at Mistress Anne again she suddenly walks across the stage with her husband, setting Wendoll off into a new paroxysm of frenzy. He literally asks to be thunderstruck on the spot. It is interesting for the actor to notice that Wendoll is not a vicious villain but comes to the role gradually and against his will. He does all he can to wrestle with his lust. In the world of this play, morality is still a strong inhibition which prevents characters from toppling over the edge too easily. Wendoll is portrayed by Heywood as a good and decent man who becomes overwhelmed by his own desires.

The Honest Whore (Part 1)
(1604) Thomas Dekker

Act 4, scene 1. Milan. A room in Hippolito's house.

Hippolito (20s), a young count, longed to marry Infeliche, the daughter of the Duke of Milan. An ancient hatred between the two houses undermined his hope of ever possessing her. She has been reported dead and as the play progresses Hippolito becomes more bitter and subject to fits of melancholy. Here his obsession with Infeliche shifts to a meditation on mortality.

HIPPOLITO *(taking a portrait).*
My Infeliche's face, her brow, her eye,
The dimple on her cheek; and such sweet skill
Hath from the cunning workman's pencil flown,
These lips look fresh and lively as her own,
Seeming to move and speak. 'Las! now I see
The reason why fond[1] women love to buy
Adulterate complexion![2] Here, 'tis read,[3]
False colours last after the true be dead.
Of all the roses grafted on her cheeks,
Of all the graces dancing in her eyes,
Of all the music set upon her tongue,
Of all that was past woman's excellence
In her white bosom – look! a painted board
Circumscribes all. Earth can no bliss afford.
Nothing of her but this? This cannot speak;
It has no lap for me to rest upon,
No lip worth tasting; here the worms will feed,

[1] **fond** foolish
[2] **Adulterate complexion** i.e. make-up
[3] **'tis read** i.e. seen in the portrait's colours

40

As in her coffin. Hence, then, idle art;
True love's best pictur'd in a true-love's heart.
Here art thou drawn, sweet maid, till this be dead;
So that thou liv'st twice, twice art buried.
Thou figure of my friend, lie there. – What's here?

Puts down portrait and takes up the skull.

Perhaps this shrewd pate was mine enemy's.
'Las! say it were; I need not fear him now!
For all his braves, his contumelious breath,[4]
His frowns, though dagger-pointed, all his plot,
Though, ne'er so mischievous, his Italian pills,
His quarrels, and that common fence,[5] his law,
See, see, they're all eaten out; here's not left one;
How clean they're pick'd away! to the bare bone!
How mad are mortals, then, to rear great names
On tops of swelling houses! or to wear out
Their fingers' ends in dirt, to scrape up gold!
Not caring so[6] that sumpter-horse,[7] the back,
Be hung with gaudy trappings, with what coarse,
Yea, rags most beggarly, they clothe the soul;
Yet, after all, their gayness looks thus foul.
What fools are men to build a garish tomb,
Only to save the carcass whilst it rots,
To maintain't long in stinking, make good carrion,
But leave no good deeds to preserve them sound;
For good deeds keep men sweet, long above ground.
And must all come to this? fools, wise, all hither?
Must all heads thus at last be laid together?
Draw me my picture then, thou grave, neat workman,
After this fashion, not like this;[8] these colours

---

[4] **contumelious breath** proud words
[5] **fence** defence
[6] **so** so that
[7] **sumpter-horse** pack-horse
[8] **this . . . this** i.e. like Infeliche's picture, not like the skull

In time, kissing but air, will be kiss'd off.
But here's a fellow; that which he lays on
Till doomsday alters not complexion.
Death's the best painter then; they that draw shapes,
And live by wicked faces, are but God's apes.
They come but near the life, and there they stay.
This fellow draws life too; his art is fuller;
The pictures which he makes are without colour.

[*lines 41–95*]

COMMENTARY: Dekker's *The Honest Whore* is a two-part play with an elaborate and exciting plot that includes three intrigues that gradually knit together. It is also at different points a comedy, a tragedy and a melodrama. In the main plot, the chaste hero Hippolito mourns the death of his beloved Infeliche. He is taken to the home of the courtesan Bellafront, whose advances he resists. She, however, falls madly in love with him and swears chastity as her new goal. When Hippolito learns that Infeliche is still alive he rushes away to marry her and Bellafront must content herself with marriage to another. The play is heavy on plot but contains some of the most lively dialogue and speeches in Jacobean drama. As this brief description suggests the full action of the play contains emotional twists and turns before all is righted in the end.

Hippolito, like Shakespeare's Romeo, lets unrequited romantic love gnaw at him like a melancholic obsession. This is a highly metaphysical speech which ingeniously uses two props to create twin poles in a debate about life and death, appearance and reality. The actor has quite a bit to manipulate in what is essentially a private rather than a public soliloquy. He must personalise both the portrait and the skull in order to achieve his dramatic effect. He catalogues the details of his love's face, trying to capture what the painter saw in the flesh. In the first part of the speech he is like a connoisseur appreciating Infeliche's delicate features as if they were a fine work of art. In the second, focusing on the skull, he is like a morbid surgeon coldly assessing mortality. There are touches of poetry hidden in this part of the speech but they fight against the darker features in the lines:

'What fools are men to build a garish tomb, / Only to save the carcass whilst it rots.' The actor might also notice that the speech sounds curiously like a sermon; it is as if Hippolito has taken on the characteristics of a celibate priest. References to time and decay run through the speech as reminders of the inevitability of death and you can perform these as solemn warnings for the benefit of the audience. Compare with Hamlet's speech on page 35.

Volpone
(1605) Ben Jonson

Act 3, scene 1. Venice. A street.

Mosca (20s–30s) is a parasite who assists Volpone, a rich and rapacious Venetian, in his grand design to dupe a host of foolish fortune-hunters out of their wealth. Mosca and Volpone are partners in crime and, as their plans succeed, Mosca begins to show signs of gleeful megalomania. This speech begins the third act and is addressed to the audience.

MOSCA.[1]
    I fear I shall begin to grow in love
    With my dear self and my most prosp'rous parts,[2]
    They do so spring and burgeon;[3] I can feel
    A whimsy[4] i' my blood. I know not how,
    Success hath made me wanton.[5] I could skip
    Out of my skin now, like a subtle[6] snake,
    I am so limber. O! your parasite
    Is a most precious thing, dropped from above,
    Not bred 'mongst clods and clodpolls, here on earth.
    I muse the mystery[7] was not made a science,[8]
    It is so liberally professed![9] Almost
    All the wise world is little else in nature

[1] **MOSCA** Italian for 'gadfly'
[2] **prosp'rous parts** flourishing talents
[3] **burgeon** expand rapidly
[4] **whimsy** giddiness
[5] **wanton** playful (with a sexual meaning)
[6] **subtle** slippery (with cunning)
[7] **mystery** craft or profession
[8] **science** field of learning
[9] **liberally professed** widely practised

But parasites or sub-parasites. And yet,
I mean not those that have your bare town-art,[10]
To know who's fit to feed 'em; have no house,
No family, no care and therefore mould
Tales[11] for men's ears, to bait that sense; or get
Kitchen-invention, and some stale receipts[12]
To please the belly, and the groin; nor those
With their court-dog tricks, that can fawn and fleer,[13]
Make their revènue out of legs and faces,[14]
Echo my lord, and lick away a moth.
But your fine, elegant rascal, that can rise
And stoop, almost together, like an arrow;
Shoot through the air as nimbly as a star;
Turn short as doth a swallow; and be here,
And there, and here, and yonder, all at once;
Present to any humour, all occasion;[15]
And change a visor[16] swifter than a thought,
This is the creature had the art born with him;
Toils not to learn it, but doth practise it
Out of most excellent nature: and such sparks
Are the true parasites, others but their zanies.[17]

[lines 1–33]

COMMENTARY: Jonson's *Volpone, or The Fox* is a classic comedy
that involves the duping of a group of legacy-hunters by a wily old
miser and his parasitical associate. Together Volpone and Mosca
invent schemes that yield a vast treasure of money, gold and
jewels. So creative are they that the plot of the play swells to fit

[10] **have . . . town-art** i.e. are streetwise
[11] **mould/Tales** spread gossip
[12] **Kitchen-invention . . . receipts** culinary invention and old recipes
[13] **fleer** smile like a sycophant
[14] **legs and faces** bowing, scraping and smiling
[15] **Present . . . occasion** seizing opportunity where it comes
[16] **visor** mask (i.e. change faces)
[17] **zanies** i.e. the comic servants in *commedia dell'arte*

their imagination. In the end their greed gets the better of them, they fall out and turn against one another, and are caught and brought to justice. Jonson conceived of the play as a kind of Aesopean beast fable with all of the characters resembling animals in their personalities and also to a certain extent in their mannerisms: Volpone is the sly fox and Mosca the buzzing gadfly. The latter aspect is something an actor can seize upon to form a characterisation.

Mosca is a superb theatrical invention who celebrates the essence of what it means to be a parasite. His appetite for mischief is insatiable. He is an energetic 'limber' thinker and acts on stage like a quick-witted improvisatory comic. You can see in this speech how acrobatic his thought process is and how he thoroughly enjoys playing his devious tricks. In fact he sees duping others as a kind of art form or 'science' and distinguishes between himself and the common variety of criminal. Mosca uses lots of slang when he speaks but is very precise and elegant in his delivery. Note how his words are slippery with 's' sounds; the verse hisses out of him like a snake. He relishes off-colour and 'wanton' images. There are numerous sexual innuendos in what he says, although he is never overtly crude. He is nimble in thought and action and can 'change a visor swifter than a thought'. His fly-like nature flits from thought to thought: 'and be here, / And there, and here, and yonder, all at once.' It is important for the actor to remember that Mosca has a higher status in Volpone's house than that of a mere servant and his role has given him airs and ambitions which grow until they finally undo him.

Coriolanus
(1607–9) William Shakespeare

Act 4, scene 5. Antium. A hall in Aufidius' house.

Coriolanus is the honorific name of the Roman general Caius Marcius (30s), who has been banished from Rome after suffering indignities and malicious accusations from the people. In characteristic outrage he turns his back on Rome, going over to the side of his enemies, the Volscians. He arrives in their capital of Antium in disguise and discovers that his rival Aufidius, General of the Volscians, is raising a new army to besiege Rome. Here Coriolanus reveals himself to Aufidius and offers him his services.

CORIOLANUS.
My name is Caius Marcius, who hath done
To thee particularly, and to all the Volsces,
Great hurt and mischief;[1] thereto witness may[2]
My surname, Coriolanus. The painful[3] service,
The extreme dangers, and the drops of blood
Shed for my thankless country, are requited
But with that surname – a good memory[4]
And witness of the malice and displeasure
Which thou shouldst bear me. Only that name remains.
The cruelty and envy[5] of the people,
Permitted by our dastard nobles, who
Have all forsook me, hath devoured the rest;
And suffered me by the voice of slaves to be

[1] **mischief** grievous wrong
[2] **witness may** you may witness
[3] **painful** arduous
[4] **memory** memorial, testimony
[5] **envy** malice

Whooped out[6] of Rome. Now, this extremity
Hath brought me to thy hearth; not out of hope –
Mistake me not – to save my life, for if
I had feared death, of all the men i' the world
I would have 'voided thee; but in mere[7] spite,
To be full quit of[8] those my banishers,
Stand I before thee here. Then if thou hast
A heart of wreak[9] in thee, that wilt revenge
Thine own particular wrongs and stop those maims
Of shame[10] seen through[11] thy country, speed thee
        straight
And make my misery serve thy turn. So use it
That my revengeful services may prove
As benefits to thee; for I will fight
Against my cankered[12] country with the spleen[13]
Of all the under fiends.[14] But if so be
Thou dar'st not this, and that to prove more fortunes[15]
Thou'rt tired, then, in a word, I also am
Longer to live most weary, and present
My throat to thee and to thy ancient[16] malice;
Which not to cut would show thee but a fool,
Since I have ever followed thee with hate,
Drawn tuns[17] of blood out of thy country's breast,
And cannot live but to thy shame, unless
It be to do thee service.   [*lines 69–104*]

---

[6] **Whooped out** driven out by jeering
[7] **mere** absolute
[8] **full quit of** fully revenged on (i.e. be quits with)
[9] **wreak** vengeance
[10] **maims / Of shame** shameful injuries (i.e. the Roman occupation of
    Corioli)
[11] **through** throughout
[12] **cankered** infected with corruption and evil
[13] **spleen** hatred, anger
[14] **under fiends** devils in hell
[15] **prove more fortunes** test your fortunes further
[16] **ancient** long-established
[17] **tuns** large barrels

COMMENTARY: *Coriolanus* is Shakespeare's last heroic tragedy. It follows on the heels of his Roman plays and features a central character who is unyielding in his anger and lust for revenge. Caius Marcius, later honoured with the title Coriolanus (to commemorate his victory over the Volscians at Corioli), is first and foremost a great warrior. When he returns to Rome scarred with victory he falls into a political struggle which his imperious temperament will not allow him either to compromise or win. He is ignominiously banished from Rome and sides with his bitter enemy and rival Aufidius to conquer the city of his birth. In the end Aufidius has him executed as a traitor.

Coriolanus is a severe and proud man. Throughout the play his colossal anger continually erupts, getting the better of him and alienating all those around him. His years on the field of battle have left him cold and callous. Only in the presence of his ambitious and politic mother Volumnia does he ever reveal a less abrasive side. In this speech he comes face to face with his worst enemy. By heaping scorn on Rome and the people he has left behind there, Coriolanus is able to come to Aufidius as an equal and not as a humble exile. Notice how strong, emphatic and challenging his words are. There are no soft phrases. Everything is harsh and blunt. The speech can be hurled like an arrogant challenge, as Coriolanus invites Aufidius to either slay him or take him in as a mercenary partner. The speech is also full of negative statements and words, all of which the actor can utter with great disdain, contempt and distaste: i.e. 'thankless country'; 'Whooped out of Rome'; etc. He is also throwing in Aufidius' face the fact that it was he who conquered Aufidius and the Volscian people at Corioli, his greatest victory. The speech is a challenge because it has to be performed in full voice in public as though it were a provocation. Remember that Coriolanus is not afraid of a fight. There is nothing manipulative, diplomatic or devious about him. He is totally upfront and uncompromising and always wears his wounds like medals of honour. Imagine how this vigorous soldier would carry himself in this scene.

The Revenger's Tragedy
(1607) Cyril Tourneur (attrib.)

Act 1, scene 1. Italy. An unnamed court.

Vindice (20s) is a malcontent still grieving over the poisoning of his beloved Gloriana, an event that happened some time before the action of the play begins. He carries her skull with him and speaks to it, adding a macabre touch to the soliloquy. It was the old, lustful Duke who performed her murder and Vindice will seek vengeance on him and his family for this deed.

VINDICE.
    Duke; royal lecher; go, grey-hair'd adultery;
    And thou his son, as impious steep'd as he;
    And thou his bastard, true-begot in evil;
    And thou his duchess, that will do with evil.
    Four excellent characters – O, that marrowless age
    Would stuff the hollow bones with damn'd desires,
    And 'stead of heat, kindle infernal fires
    Within the spendthrift veins of a dry duke,
    A parch'd and juiceless luxur.[1] O God! – one
    That has scarce blood enough to live upon,
    And he to riot it[2] like a son and heir?
    O, the thought of that
    Turns my abused heart strings into fret.
    Thou sallow picture of my poison'd love,
    My study's ornament, thou shell of death,
    Once the bright face of my betrothed lady,
    When life and beauty naturally fill'd out
    These ragged imperfections,

[1] **luxur** a lover of lust
[2] **riot it** act debauched

When two heaven-pointed diamonds were set
In those unsightly rings – then 'twas a face
So far beyond the artificial shine
Of any woman's bought complexion,[3]
That the uprightest man (if such there be
That sin but seven times a day) broke custom,
And made up eight with looking after her.
O, she was able to ha' made a usurer's son
Melt all his patrimony in a kiss,
And what his father fifty years told,
To have consum'd, and yet his suit been cold.
But O, accursed palace!
Thee when thou wert apparel'd in thy flesh
The old duke poison'd,
Because thy purer part would not consent
Unto his palsy-lust; for old men lustful
Do show like young men, angry, eager, violent,
Outbid like their limited performances.
O 'ware an old man hot and vicious:
Age, as in gold, in lust is covetous.
Vengeance, thou murder's quit-rent,[4] and whereby
Thou show'st thyself tenant to Tragedy,
O, keep thy day, hour, minute, I beseech,
For those thou hast determin'd![5] – hum, who e'er knew
Murder unpaid? Faith, give Revenge her due,
Sh' has kept touch hitherto – be merry, merry,
Advance thee, O thou terror to fat folks,
To have their costly three-pil'd flesh worn off
As bare as this – for banquets, ease and laughter,
Can make great men, as greatness goes by clay;
But wise men little are more great than they.

[*lines 1–49*]

---

[3] **bought complexion** i.e. artificially made up
[4] **quit-rent** a small amount paid to a landlord for services
[5] **determin'd** put to their end (i.e. killed)

COMMENTARY: *The Revenger's Tragedy*, attributed to Cyril Tourneur, is one of the darkest and most morbid of the Jacobean revenge plays. Even the 'hero' of the play, Vindice (pronounced *Vin-dee'-chee*), is consumed by evil and passion for revenge. The plot of the play concerns his long-sought vengeance on the Duke who poisoned Gloriana, Vindice's betrothed. Wild confusion and multiple murders fill the labyrinthian action. In the end Vindice exacts his revenge but is sentenced to death by the new Duke.

Vindice opens the play spitting out accusations and curses at each member of the Duke's family as they pass before him, though he remains unseen and unheard. Old unsettled accounts suddenly come back to life. He next speaks to the skull of his beloved Gloriana which he always carries with him like a *memento mori*. This is an extremely useful prop for an actor and allows him to personalise the speech and bring the past into the present. Obviously everything that was once beautiful and pure has now become corrupted and decayed in Vindice's brooding mind. His imagination can only dwell on vengeance and death. He is a man obsessed and consumed by revenge. He uses the skull as a constant means of prompting him to act. Vindice has isolated himself from the court and in the world of this kind of play, full of claustrophobia and insulated from the world at large, being on the outside is like being dead. So Vindice assumes a new role as a railing malcontent. Much of the speech focuses on diseased appearances and signals how diseased Vindice's mind has become. Although the actor should not stoop to comedy in this speech, the monologue is full of black humour, puns, wordplay and ironies which ought to be enjoyed.

The Alchemist
(1610) Ben Jonson

Act 2, scene 2. London. A room in Lovewit's house.

Sir Epicure Mammon (30s–40s), a knight, visits Subtle, the alchemist, in the hopes of having his base goods transformed into gold. He is a covetous and vain gentleman who is 'slow of his feet, but earnest of his tongue.' Here he describes to Subtle's companion Face what he will do with his anticipated wealth.

SIR EPICURE MAMMON.
　Lungs,[1] I will set a period[2]
To all thy labours; thou shalt be the master
Of my seraglio[3] . . . For I do mean
To have a list of wives and concubines
Equal with Solomon, who had the Stone[4]
Alike with me; and I will make me a back[5]
With the elixir, that shall be as tough
As Hercules, to encounter fifty a night –
Th'art sure thou saw'st it blood? –
I will have all my beds blown up, not stuffed:
Down is too hard; and then, mine oval room
Filled with such pictures[6] as Tiberius took
From Elephantis, and dull Aretine
But coldly imitated. Then, my glasses
Cut in more subtle angles, to disperse

---

[1] **Lungs** i.e. Face (referred to as if he were an alchemist's fire bellows)
[2] **period** goal
[3] **seraglio** sultan's palace
[4] **Stone** i.e. the philosopher's stone, the magical elixir that was the object of the alchemist's search
[5] **a back** i.e. my back (sexual allusion)
[6] **pictures** i.e. pornographic paintings

And multiply the figures, as I walk
Naked between my *succubae*.[7] My mists
I'll have of perfume, vapoured 'bout the room,
To lose our selves in; and my baths, like pits
To fall into, from whence we will come forth,
And roll us dry in gossamer and roses –
Is it arrived at ruby? – Where I spy
A wealthy citizen, or rich lawyer,
Have a sublimed, pure wife, unto that fellow
I'll send a thousand pound to be my cuckold.
                . . . No, I'll ha' no bawds[8]
But fathers and mothers – they will do it best,
Best of all others. And my flatterers
Shall be the pure and gravest of divines
That I can get for money. My mere fools
Eloquent burgesses,[9] and then my poets
The same that writ so subtly of the fart,
Whom I will entertain still for that subject.
The few that would give out themselves to be
Court- and town-stallions[10] and each-where bely[11]
Ladies who are known most innocent, for them,
These will I beg, to make me eunuchs of,
And they shall fan me with ten estrich tails
Apiece, made in a plume to gather wind.
We will be brave,[12] Puff, now we ha' the med'cine.
My meat shall all come in, in Indian shells,
Dishes of agate set in gold, and studded
With emeralds, sapphires, hyacinths, [13] and rubies.
The tongues of carps, dormice, and camels' heels,

---

[7] **succubae** i.e. concubines
[8] **bawds** i.e. pimps
[9] **burgesses** high-minded citizens
[10] **stallions** male prostitutes
[11] **each-where bely** everywhere slander
[12] **brave** splendid
[13] **hyacinths** precious stone

Boiled i' the spirit of Sol,[14] and dissolved pearl
(Apicius'[15] diet, 'gainst the epilepsy);
And I will eat these broths with spoons of amber,
Headed with diamond and carbuncle.
My foot-boy shall eat pheasants, calvered[16] salmons,
Knots, godwits, lampreys.[17] I myself will have
The beards of barbels[18] served instead of salads;
Oiled mushrooms; and the swelling unctuous paps
Of a fat pregnant sow, newly cut off,
Dressed with an exquisite and poignant sauce;
For which, I'll say unto my cook, 'There's gold;
Go forth, and be a knight!'

[*lines 32–87*]

COMMENTARY: Jonson's *The Alchemist* is a comic exposition on different forms of greed. Two con-men, Subtle and Face, dupe an assortment of fortune-hunters who hope to benefit from Subtle's supposed alchemical skills. He promises to turn all their base metals into gold. Chief among the characters who come to their door is Sir Epicure Mammon. As his name implies he is the man with the biggest appetite of all. In a series of soliloquies he fantasises on what his anticipated riches will bring him. He continually comes to the house to check on the alchemical process. Like all the others he is duped and ends up losing everything.

This is one of the most extravagant speeches in Elizabethan drama. Sir Epicure's greediness and voluptuousness are transformed into images and allusions that are grossly sensual and repellent in their excess. He is standing about waiting for the Philosopher's Stone to turn bright red – 'thou saw'st it blood?' and 'Is it arrived at ruby?' – at which point all his dreams of gold

[14] **spirit of Sol** gold
[15] **Apicius** a legendary Roman epicurean
[16] **calvered** carved while still alive
[17] **Knots, godwits, lampreys** all types of birds
[18] **barbels** a carp-like fish

will be alchemically assured. Notice how his mouth waters in anticipation of the delicacies to come, some of which are so fantastical that they defy coherent understanding. The actor must imagine all the possibilities that these words signify for such a sensualist. Sir Epicure is excitedly building up an appetite to feast all his senses once he possesses his gold but what he describes is sheer gluttony. In his imagination food and sexual delight constantly intersect and become synonymous. As a speaker he engages in hyperbole and the actor will want to exploit this as fully as possible. Note how specific he is in his choice of delicious images; he will not just eat common game birds, but must have 'knots, godwits, lampreys'. When you read this speech on the page it may seem complex; when you speak it out loud it can be truly relished. It must not be rushed through but should be savoured for all its verbal flavours as though you were enjoying a wonderful banquet. Notice how concentrated and contained the verse is; although the images are extravagant the lines are very tightly controlled.

The White Devil
(1612) John Webster

Act 5, scene 4. Padua. A room in the palace.

Flamineo (20s), the ambitious and unscrupulous brother of Vittoria Corombona, has procured his sister for the Duke of Brachiano. Under orders from the Duke, Flamineo then commits the double murders of both Vittoria's husband and the Duke's wife. After a quarrel he treacherously murders his own brother in the presence of his mother who is driven mad with grief. Here Flamineo ruminates on his prospects, anticipating a rich reward from his sister for his villainy. Meanwhile the Duke has been killed in revenge for the murder of his wife by her relatives and here appears to Flamineo as a ghost.

FLAMINEO.
    This night I'll know the utmost of my fate,
    I'll be resolv'd what my rich sister means
    T'assign me for my service. I have liv'd
    Riotously ill, like some that live in court.
    And sometimes, when my face was full of smiles
    Have felt the maze of conscience in my breast.
    Oft gay and honour'd robes those tortures try,[1]
    'We think cag'd birds sing, when indeed they cry.'

Enter Brachiano's Ghost. In his leather cassock and breeches, boots, a cowl and in his hand a pot of lily-flowers with a skull in't.

    Ha! I can stand thee. Nearer, nearer yet.
    What a mockery hath death made of thee? Thou look'st
      sad.

[1] **Oft . . . try** i.e. qualms of conscience often test the value and integrity of great men in their fine robes

In what place art thou? in yon starry gallery,
Or in the cursed dungeon? No? not speak?
Pray, sir, resolve me, what religion's best
For a man to die in? or is it in your knowledge
To answer me how long I have to live?
That's the most necessary question.
Not answer? Are you still like some great men
That only walk like shadows up and down,
And to no purpose: say:

The Ghost throws earth upon him and shows him the skull.

What's that? O fatal! He throws earth upon me.
A dead man's skull beneath the roots of flowers.
I pray speak sir; our Italian churchmen
Make us believe, dead men hold conference
With their familiars,[2] and many times
Will come to bed to them, and eat with them.

Exit Ghost.

He's gone; and see, the skull and earth are vanish'd.
This is beyond melancholy. I do dare my fate
To do its worst. Now to my sister's lodging,
And sum up all these horrors; the disgrace
The Prince threw on me; next the pitious sight
Of my dead brother; and my mother's dotage;
And last this terrible vision. All these
Shall with Vittoria's bounty turn to good,
Or I will drown this weapon in her blood.

[*lines 126–159*]

---

[2] **familiars** familiar spirits; friends or relations

COMMENTARY: Webster's *The White Devil* is a tale of jealousy and death in which the beautiful Vittoria Corombona encourages the affections of the Duke of Brachiano which eventually lead to the murder of her husband Camillo. The love affair and murder are partly engineered by her diabolical brother Flamineo, who also plots the death of Brachiano's wife Isabella. A whirlwind of passions and revenge follow from these incidents as all three characters die ignominiously in the end along with a host of other characters.

Flamineo is one of the most cold-blooded and resolute villains in Jacobean drama. Neither morality nor family ties stop him from committing crime after crime. This speech is a momentary interruption in his murderous vendetta and although far from being a confession it is as close as Flamineo comes to suffering a crisis of conscience. The madness of his mother touches something inside him and causes him to reflect on his evil ways. His dialogue with the ghost is full of questions which must remain unanswered and you must decide if he is waiting for answers or merely challenging the ghost with a barrage of questions. The ghost gives him an intimation of his death to come. For the actor, one surprising aspect of the speech is that the character seems more curious of the spectre than frightened of it. He is cocky and challenging, proud of his shrewdness and cynicism. Throughout the play he has been a calculating and plotting Machiavellian villain and by this point in the action Flamineo is so steeped in blood and treachery that he barely knows the difference between right and wrong. He accepts anything that comes his way. As soon as the ghost disappears and he brushes the dirt away he is back into the action, and off in pursuit of his sister. Notice how simple and direct the language is, completely lacking in rhetorical flourishes. One of Flamineo's strengths as a character is that he lacks all affectations and knows exactly what he is and what he wants.

The Changeling

(*c.* 1622) Thomas Middleton & William Rowley

Act 2, scene 1. Spain. A room in the castle at Alicante.

De Flores (20s–30s) is a manservant to the Governor of Alicante and is renowned for his ugliness. He is fatally attracted to the Governor's beautiful daughter, Beatrice-Joanna, who cannot bear the sight of him. This does not stop him from desiring her.

DE FLORES.
                            Yonder's she;
Whatever ails me, now a' late especially,
I can as well be hang'd as refrain seeing her;
Some twenty times a day, nay, not so little,
Do I force errands, frame ways and excuses,
To come into her sight; and I've small reason for't,
And less encouragement; for she baits[1] me still
Every time worse than other, does profess herself
The cruellest enemy to my face in town,
At no hand[2] can abide the sight of me,
As if danger or ill luck hung in my looks.
I must confess my face is bad enough,
But I know far worse has better fortune,
And not endur'd alone, but doted on;
And yet such pick-hair'd faces,[3] chins like witches',
Here and there five hairs whispering in a corner,
As if they grew in fear one of another,
Wrinkles like troughs, where swine-deformity swills
The tears of perjury, that lie there like wash

[1] **baits** entices
[2] **At no hand** in no way whatsoever
[3] **pick-hair'd faces** i.e. faces covered with hair like hedgehog spines

60

Fallen from the slimy and dishonest eye, –
Yet such a one plucks sweets without restraint,
And has the grace of beauty to his sweet.[4]
Though my hard fate has thrust me out to servitude,
I tumbled into th' world a gentleman.
She turns her blessed eye upon me now,
And I'll endure all storms before I part with 't.

[lines 26–51]

COMMENTARY: *The Changeling* is one of the most powerful and unremitting of the Jacobean revenge tragedies. At its centre is a psychological study of a capricious young woman who gradually 'changes' from an innocent to a victimiser to a victim as the result of a sudden crime of passion. The relationship between Beatrice-Joanna and the grotesque De Flores is the story of beauty and the beast. De Flores worships her from afar and then takes control over her when he murders on her behalf. The tragedy continually progresses from bad to worse as the two oddly matched 'lovers' die in a double death. Madness and sexual passion propel the action.

De Flores is speaking about Beatrice-Joanna in an aside while she stands elsewhere on stage observing him, so his speech must be spoken confidentially. It is a rather simple speech and the main objective is to show the eagerness and delight at the sight of the other character, at the same time keeping it hidden. He is drawn to her, does everything he can to force an encounter with her and is supremely happy when he is in her presence. She is exactly what he is not: physically attractive. He is described as having 'a hairy, pimply, dog face'. The way that De Flores goes on about his ugliness seems almost sado-masochistic. He dwells on it at such length that he increases the horror for us. He knows his face in precise detail and treats it like a map of some pock-marked terrain. His self-loathing is almost celebratory. Notice the lines about the hairs on his face which are so grotesque they seem comic. His outward state reflects his inner being which is equally twisted and distorted and the actor should notice that each of his

[4] **sweet** sweetheart's eyes

61

lines is full of self-deprecation and resentment. In a play that has so much to do with 'change' De Flores is incapable of changing the one thing – his appearance – that he most wants to change. This speech establishes his immutability early on.

'Tis Pity She's a Whore
(1625–33) John Ford

Act 1, scene 2. Parma. A street.

Giovanni (18–20), the brilliant son of Florio and brother to the beautiful Annabella, has confessed to Friar Bonaventura, his former university tutor, that he is infatuated with his own sister. The friar has advised Giovanni to go home and give himself up to prayer. In this scene Giovanni wanders the streets in a state of despair at his incestuous desires.

GIOVANNI.
  Lost, I am lost. My fates have doomed my death.
  The more I strive, I love; the more I love,
  The less I hope: I see my ruin, certain.
  What judgement or endeavours could apply
  To my incurable and restless wounds
  I throughly[1] have examined, but in vain.
  O that it were not in religion sin
  To make our love a god, and worship it.
  I have even wearied Heaven with prayers, dried up
  The spring of my continual tears, even starved
  My veins with daily fasts: what wit or art
  Could counsel, I have practised: but alas,
  I find all these but dreams and old men's tales
  To fright unsteady youth; I'm still the same.
  Or[2] I must speak, or burst. 'Tis not, I know,
  My lust, but 'tis my fate that leads me on.

[1] **throughly** i.e. thoroughly
[2] **Or** Either

Keep fear and low faint-hearted shame with slaves;
I'll tell her that I love her, though my heart
Were rated[3] at the price of that attempt.
O me! She comes.

Enter Annabella and her maid.

[*lines 150–169*]

COMMENTARY: Ford's *'Tis Pity She's a Whore* follows the
fortunes of two star-crossed lovers who happen to be brother and
sister. It is a kind of profane *Romeo and Juliet* in which incest
replaces chasteness. The incestuous coupling happens quite early
in the first act (soon after this speech) and the rest of the play
becomes a delayed reaction to this disastrous mating. Both lovers
die in the end but not before the entire society depicted in the
play is shattered. In the final scene Giovanni enters with
Annabella's heart on the end of his dagger.

Giovanni is one of the most impulsive and fiery young men in
Jacobean drama. An actor has to decide for himself just how
moral or amoral he is within the system of belief set up in this
play. Giovanni is almost primitive in nature, although highly
educated, and has evolved a philosophical system all his own. The
first part of the play shows him in debate with Friar Bonaventura
over what are essentially anti-Christian sentiments. He is truly a
'lost' man, an outsider and a renegade for whom incest becomes a
symbolic expression of his revolt. Notice how he uses antithesis to
signal his warring tensions: 'The more I strive, I love; the more I
love, the less I hope.' For a character like Giovanni, two sides of
himself are always in conflict, but it is never clear which is the
better half. There is also the physical attraction to his sister which
drives him in the direction of lust. He has done everything he can
to resist this temptation, but the inclination only gets stronger
and stronger. He believes he is ruled by a kind of elemental fate
and having accepted this he lets his fate lead him on. Giovanni is a
brilliant sceptic, as intellectual and capable with language and
ideas as Hamlet. The actor playing him must use as much
imaginative energy as possible to capture the overweening

[3] **rated** measured

restlessness of his intelligence. Notice that he already knows he is doomed – there is a kind of freedom and release that comes as a result of this recognition. Notice, too, that Giovanni is sarcastic in the face of fate. His character is fuelled by a bitterness towards all conventions which he seeks to destroy and in the end he will do everything he can to flaunt his transgression of this most serious of all taboos. In Act Five, after he has killed Annabella, he enters a banquet brandishing her heart on the end of his dagger and taunts all present: 'Fate or all the powers / That guide the motions of immortal souls / Could not prevent me.'

Life is a Dream

(1635) Calderón [Pedro Calderón de la Barca]

Act 2. Poland. The interior of a tower on a craggy mountain top.

Segismundo (20s) is the legitimate heir to the throne of Poland. He was locked in a tower by his father King Basilio when a horoscope cast at his birth said that he would seize the throne and rule like a tyrant. As a test, Basilio has him drugged and put temporarily on the throne to see if the prophecy proves to be correct. He does become a cruel tyrant and in the second act of the play is sent back to the tower and to his captive state. Never sure if he is awake or dreaming, Segismundo in his despair delivers this philosophical speech.

SEGISMUNDO (*shackled in chains and dressed in animal skins*).

I must control this savagery,
This wild ambition, this ferocity
Of mine in case I dream again.
For surely I'll dream again
When this world seems so strange a place
That all our life is but a dream,
And what I've seen so far tells me
That any man who lives dreams what
He is until at last he wakes.
The King dreams he is king and so
Believing rules, administers,
Rejoices in the exercise of power;
He does not seem to know his fame
Is written on the wind and death
Will turn to ashes all his splendour.
O who would want to be a king
And have his power, when the dream

Of death must soon awaken him?
The rich man dreams in all his wealth,
Though riches cause him endless care.
The pauper dreams his suffering,
Complaining that the world's not fair.
The man who has success dreams too,
And so does he who strives for more.
He dreams whose heart is full of spite,
Who, hurting others, claims he's right.
The world, in short, is where men dream
The different parts that they are playing,
And no one stops to know their meaning.
I dream that I am here, a prisoner,
I dream that I am bound by chains,
When once I dreamt of palaces
Where I was king, where once I reigned.
What is this life? A fantasy?
A prize we seek so eagerly
That proves to be illusory?
I think that life is but a dream,
And even dreams not what they seem.

Translated by Gwynne Edwards

COMMENTARY: Calderón's *Life is a Dream* starts as a tragedy and ends as an uplifting lesson about man's capacity to exercise his own free will. Segismundo, heir to the throne of Poland, begins the action chained in a tower like a beast. At his birth a prophecy decreed that he would be a tyrant if allowed to become king. As a result his father King Basilio had him immediately imprisoned in the tower. However, King Basilio plans to abdicate his throne in favour of his nephew Astolfo, Duke of Moscow. Before committing himself he decides to test Segismundo by putting him on the throne for a trial period of rule. Drugged and sleeping, he is taken from his prison and awakens to all the splendour of a baroque palace. With the ferocity of a caged animal suddenly set free, he lashes out and tyrannises everyone around him, seeming to prove the prophecy. Drugged once again, he is returned to his tower and awakens to ponder what it has all meant in one of the most celebrated speeches in Spanish drama. Soon afterwards Segismundo is liberated from his tower again and, having learned his lesson well, harnesses his temper and rules like a model prince.

Segismundo's whole life has been spent chained in a tower isolated from all human contact. A sudden taste of unexpected freedom, coupled with his experience of life as little more than a caged creature, confuse and prevent him from acting like a civilised man. He acts out of instinct and not by intellect: one of the play's main propositions. Having the chance to reflect on all that has happened to him, he ponders one of the central questions of drama: is life a dream or a reality? Are we not all actors in some universal play? The speech is structured like an internal debate. It is exactly the same kind of soliloquy that Hamlet delivers. While the bestial side of Segismundo was on display earlier in the play (he killed several of the courtiers who stood in his way) here his reflective capacity fuels the scene. The metaphysical nature of the speech cannot be abstract for the actor; it must come from some kind of experience of what the character has lived through thus far. Segismundo, like Hamlet, is an intuitive philosopher who ruminates and activates rumination into speech. Notice what a restless mind he has as he continually pits one element against another so that prisons and palaces become separate poles of an entire life experience. Note, too, that most of the lines are in eight syllables, creating a rhythmic scheme that should carry you through the speech. This is not naturalistic language and the actor must give the verse its due as it gradually grows to a conclusion.

The Misanthrope
(1666) Molière [Jean Baptiste Poquelin]

Act 1, scene 1. Paris. A salon in Célimène's house.

Alceste (30s), a misanthrope with a vast distaste for the hypocrisy he sees rampant in society, begins the play speaking to his more moderate friend Philinte. Alceste believes that plain speaking should be the order of the day and nothing incites him more than people who fawn and are two-faced. Here he expresses some of his uncompromising views of mankind.

ALCESTE.
> No, I include all men in one dim view:
> Some men I hate for being rogues; the others
> I hate because they treat the rogues like brothers,
> And, lacking a virtuous scorn for what is vile,
> Receive the villain with a complaisant smile.
> Notice how tolerant people choose to be
> Toward that bold rascal who's at law with me.
> His social polish can't conceal his nature;
> One sees at once that he's a treacherous creature;
> No one could possibly be taken in
> By those soft speeches and that sugary grin.
> The whole world knows the shady means by which
> The low-brow's grown so powerful and rich,
> And risen to a rank so bright and high
> That virtue can but blush, and merit sigh.
> Whenever his name comes up in conversation,
> None will defend his wretched reputation;
> Call him knave, liar, scoundrel, and all the rest,
> Each head will nod, and no one will protest.
> And yet his smirk is seen in every house,
> He's greeted everywhere with smiles and bows,

And when there's any honour that can be got
By pulling strings, he'll get it, like as not.
My God! It chills my heart to see the ways
Men come to terms with evil nowadays;
Sometimes, I swear, I'm moved to flee and find
Some desert land unfouled by humankind.

Translated by Richard Wilbur

COMMENTARY: Molière's *The Misanthrope* is one of the great studies of comic character in world drama. Alceste is self-righteously opposed to the superficiality of the society in which he lives and to some degree he is right. The world in which he moves is full of gossip, slander, lawsuits and false love and Alceste is himself being sued in the courts for libel, which only compounds his misanthropy. He is in love with Célimène whose flirtatiousness with other men and tolerance of society's foibles only adds to his despair. She is his comic flaw and their incompatibility leads to his departure from Paris at the end of the play on a very sour note.

The speech is written entirely in rhyming couplets, as is the whole play. They are not to be spoken preciously or too poetically. Use the rhymes as a sarcastic weapon. In fact, the rhyming should sound spontaneous, exactly as if the character is minting the thought as he speaks it. Alceste is all-encompassing in his hatred of mankind. The play gives no psychological reason for this, except that Alceste lives in a world in which he, as his friend Philinte says, is the odd man out. What he rails against is human imperfection. The actor should just take Alceste's convictions at face value and enter into his obsession. Go through the play and list all the things that irritate him. When you perform the speech notice how Alceste likes to use words that sound like sneers 'complaisant smile', 'treacherous creature', 'wretched reputation', 'shady means', 'sugary grin', etc. These are real gifts for an actor to speak and they allow you to arrive at a character very quickly. Throughout the play Alceste has many more speeches just like this one and they bring him into instant conflict with every other character in the play. He is stubborn and contrary to any opinion except his own. Ultimately he is the cause of his own undoing.

The Miser
(1668) Molière [Jean Baptiste Poquelin]

Act 4, scene 7. Paris. A room in Harpagon's house.

Harpagon (50s) is a widowed father with a son and daughter of marriageable age. He is absolutely governed by his miserliness. He hoards his wealth zealously and leads a life of comically mean parsimony, suspecting that everyone, including his family and his loyal servants, is out to get his money. He has just discovered that his treasure box filled with 10,000 pieces of gold, which he had buried in his garden, is missing.

HARPAGON.
Stop thief! Robber! Assassin! Murderer! Give me justice, Heaven, justice. I'm done for. I'm killed. They've slit my throat; they've run off with my money! Who did it! What's become of him? Where's he got to? Where is he now? Where's he hiding? How can I find him? Which way to go – this way or that? Is he here? Is he there? Who's that? Stop. Give me back my money. (*Grabs his own arm.*) Ah, oh, it's me. I'm going mad! I don't know where I am, who I am or what I'm doing. O my poor money, my poor, poor money, my dearest friend, you've been taken away from me. I've lost my strength, my comfort, my joy. Without you what's the point in going on? It's the end, it's all over now. I'm dying. I'm dead. I'm buried. Is there no one who can resurrect me by returning my gold? Isn't there anyone who'll tell me who took it? What? What, did somebody say something? – There's no one there. Whoever did it must have been watching me round the clock and picked that moment just as I was talking with that wretch of a son of mine. I'll call in the magistrates. I'll have the whole

household tortured – servants, maids, son, daughter, all of them – me too. What a crew! I suspect them all – they all look guilty. What's that? What are they saying? Is my thief there too? I beg you, if you know anything, on bended knees, just to tell me. Is he hiding there among you? Oops. Now they're all staring at me and laughing. Oh I get it. I see – they're all involved in this – all conspirators. Come on, hurry up. Where are they then? I want police, watchmen, magistrates, torturers and hangmen. I'll have the whole lot hanged, and if I don't get my money back then I'll hang myself too!

COMMENTARY: Molière's *The Miser* is a prose comedy that is among the best of his full-length comedies of character. It focuses on the miserly Harpagon and his rivalry with his son Cléante for the hand of the young Mariane, and on a second plot involving the secret love of his daughter Elise and Harpagon's steward Valère. By marrying his daughter to old Anselme, Harpagon hopes to secure yet another fortune. The action of the play not only revolves around money but also involves a battle of wills between generations. Much of the plot and the characters are drawn from the stock situations and types found in the Italian *commedia dell'arte*, although Molière's dialogue and characterisation are much more memorable. By the end of the play Harpagon has been outwitted and defrauded and a cruel residue hangs over the finale.

Harpagon's violent outburst at the loss of his gold is so excessive it seems as if he has been mortally wounded. And so he has. Gold for Harpagon is part of his very essence. It is as though he has just suffered the kidnapping or murder of a precious child, especially since the gold means so much more to him than either of his two children. Notice how fragmented and distracted the whole speech is. He is in a state of shock and delirium. You can imagine he is searching the entire stage for clues and suspects; indeed, his suspicions even include the audience. Harpagon is so consumed by his monstrous greed that the speech should really come across as a shocking neurotic diatribe. There is nothing overtly hilarious about him; he is a fanatical, excessive character whose meanness extends to every area of his domestic life. The savagery with which he has treated every member of his household has been strict and severe. In his frenzy he is prepared to prosecute and hang the entire world, himself included. What's the point of living once you've lost your gold? You cannot play Harpagon without tapping the very dark centre of this character. This is not lightweight comedy, but Molière's special brand of deadly serious humour which exposes the nightmare side of human folly.

Phedra
(1677) Jean Racine

Act 2. Troezen (a city near Athens). Somewhere in the palace.

*Hippolytus (18–20) is the son of Theseus, King of Athens, who is
believed to be dead. He is in love with Aricia, a captive princess and
here he declares his passion for her. She believes he hates her, but in
this speech he reveals that his passion is that of a man mortally in love.*

HIPPOLYTUS.
   No: I am stepped in too far.
   I see that reason's forced to yield to passion's violence;
   But, Madam, since I am in the way to break my silence,
   I cannot choose but to continue and unfold
   The secret hidden in my heart: you must be told.
   Look at me, pity me if you can, if not, deride
   This fallen monument to overweening pride;
   A pride that scorned the feebleness of men in love,
   Kissing the flimsy fetters they were captives of.
   I've seen men shipwrecked in the storms of love, and
         swore
   I would forever watch such tempests from the shore.
   Now, subjugated to the common law of Nature,
   I do not recognise myself in any feature.
   A single moment wrecked my reckless, raw conceit;
   Pride went before a fall; my downfall was complete.
   For half a year, ashamed and desperate, I've tried
   Vainly to dislodge the weapon in my side.
   I fly your presence, vainly rail against myself and you;
   But even in your absence, your image still shows
         through.
   In the dark forest's depths, still I can see your face;

74

No matter what the hour, day, time, occasion, place,
All mirrors the enchantments which I try to shun,
Delivering at your feet, my failed rebellion.
And all the poor regard of my superfluous care,
Is that I seek myself, and find myself – nowhere.
My bow, my spears all rust: my chariot stands idle;
My horses have forgot the touch of bit and bridle,
As I myself now quite neglect their management,
In the dark forests where my cheerless days are spent.
My love makes me a savage: do you blush to learn
The nature of the wheel on which you make me turn?
Strange words perhaps from one who only longs to be
Led to the sacrifice in soft captivity.
I'm speaking in a language I'm unpractised in;
Accept the love I offer as no less genuine
For being ill-expressed, and do not be aggrieved
By words which, but for you, I could not have conceived.

[*lines 494–530*]
Translated by Robert David MacDonald

COMMENTARY: Racine's *Phedra* is one of the most unrelenting of the great classical tragedies. All of the characters are victims of Fate and the hatred of the gods. Phedra, wife of Theseus, herself the daughter of Minos and a descendant of the Sun, is passionately in love with her stepson Hippolytus. Her feelings of guilt are overwhelming. Hippolytus is in love with Aricia and is shocked when he learns of Phedra's passion for him. The sudden return of Theseus, who was believed dead, sends the tragedy spiralling to its disastrous conclusion. Through their monologues and dialogues all of the characters express a torment that is unbearable. Death is almost a welcome relief from the pounding tension.

Hippolytus' confession is like one long torture. Notice how physically distressing it is for him. This is a man who is no longer himself and who has lost his ability to reason. Words like 'fall' and 'fallen' point the direction in which Hippolytus is heading. Although a great warrior he is unprotected when it comes to love and he describes himself as being lost in a forest and in captivity.

Practically all of the lines are end-stopped, meaning that the energy of the speech is contained in each of the separate lines of verse. English cannot duplicate or adequately translate the sound and poetic power of the twelve-syllable French alexandrine with its climactic break in each line. You must try to remember that each sentence is a separate unit of energy that, like a series of waves, gets stronger and stronger as the tide of passion breaks against the shore. The effect should be of unrelenting power that builds and builds.

The Country Wife
(1675) William Wycherley

Act 4, scene 3. London. A room in Pinchwife's house.

Mr Pinchwife (40s–50s) has recently married a naïve country girl who he has brought to London and he is determined to protect her from the rakes of the town. Horner, the most ingenious of these, after seeing Margery plans to conquer her. Pinchwife has forced his wife to write Horner a dismissive letter. He comes into the room to find her writing to Horner on her own and snatches the paper from her to read it out loud.

PINCHWIFE.
What, writing more letters? . . . How's this! nay you shall not stir Madam.

Deare, Deare, deare, Mr Horner – very well – I have taught you to write letters to good purpose – but let's see't.

First I am to beg your pardon for my boldness in writing to you, which I'd have you to know, I would not have done, had not you said first you lov'd me so extremely, which if you do, you will never suffer me to lie in the arms of another man, whom I loath, nauseate, and detest – [Now you can write these filthy words] but what follows – Therefore I hope you will speedily find some way to free me from this unfortunate match, which was never, I assure you, of my choice, but I'm afraid 'tis already too far gone; however if you love me, as I do you, you will try what you can do, but you must help me away before to morrow, or else alas I shall be for ever out of your reach, for I can defer no longer our – our – (*The letter concludes.*) what is to follow our – speak what? our journey into the country I suppose – Oh woman, damn'd woman, and love, damn'd love, their old tempter, for this is one of his miracles, in a moment, he can make those blind that cou'd see, those dumb that could speak, and those prattle who were dumb before, nay what is more than all, make these dow-bak'd,[1] senseless, indocile[2] animals, Women, too hard for us their politick lords and rulers in a moment; But make an end of your letter, and then I'll make an end of you thus, and all my plagues together. (*Draws his sword.*)

COMMENTARY: Wycherley's *The Country Wife* was written at a time when love and wenching were the business of drama. It concerns Horner, a libertine, who pretends to be impotent in order to divest suspicious husbands of their wives. It seems that every female in London is willing to be seduced by Horner, even the naïve country wife of Mr Pinchwife. It is full of licentious moments and frank talk about sex and seduction. The play also pits the manners of the city against those of the country.

Mr Pinchwife is the classic cuckold: no matter what he does to protect himself he will always be gulled and outwitted by people like Mr Horner. This scene is a case in point. He has taught his wife Margery how to write so that she will send letters rebuffing Horner's advances, but she does quite the opposite. The character's anger is lit by the reading of the letter which acts as a fuse until he explodes and draws his sword. Notice that he reads the letter without taking any of the full stops, in one breathless wave of words. In fact the actor could wisely play with the character's breathlessness since he must surely lose control at some point. Although Pinchwife is the very caricature of a cuckold it is not in the actor's interest to play this too broadly. Think instead of an older man obsessively consumed by jealousy for his younger wife. The letter also reveals just how much Margery detests him.

[1] **dow-bak'd** feeble minded
[2] **indocile** unteachable

78

The Rover (Part 1)
(1678) Aphra Behn

Act 3, scene 3. Naples at carnival time. A street.

Blunt (20s), an English country gentleman and banished Cavalier, gets caught up in the Naples carnival and takes up with the prostitute Lucetta. He has just escaped from her trap by means of a common sewer from which he emerges practically naked and completely filthy. This is what he has to say about the whole escapade.

BLUNT.
Oh Lord! (*Climbing up.*) I am got out at last, and (which is a miracle) without a clue[1] – and now to damning and cursing, – but if that would ease me, where shall I begin? with my fortune, my self, or the Quean[2] that cozen'd[3] me – What a dog was I to believe in Women! Oh Coxcomb[4] – ignorant conceited Coxcomb! to fancy she cou'd be enamour'd with my person, at the first sight enamour'd – Oh, I'm a cursed puppy, 'tis plain, Fool was writ upon my forehead, she perceiv'd it, – saw the Essex Calf[5] there – for what allurements could there be in this countenance? which I can endure, because I'm acquainted with it – Oh, dull silly dog! to be thus sooth'd[6] into a Cozening! Had I been drunk, I might fondly have credited the young Quean! but as I was in my right wits, to be thus cheated, confirms I am a dull believing English Country Fop. – But my comrades! Death and the Devil, there's the worst of all – then a ballad will be

[1] **clue** trail
[2] **Quean** prostitute
[3] **cozen'd** tricked
[4] **Coxcomb** fool
[5] **Essex Calf** (a term of contempt)
[6] **sooth'd** cajoled

sung to morrow on the *Prado*, to a lousy[7] tune of the enchanted squire, and the annihilated damsel – But Fred that rogue, and the Colonel, will abuse me beyond all Christian patience – had she left me my clothes, I have a bill of exchange at home, wou'd have sav'd my credit – but now all hope is taken from me – Well, I'll home (if I can find the way) with this consolation, that I am not the first kind believing Coxcomb; but there are, Gallants, many such good natures amongst ye.

> And tho you've better Arts to hide your Follies,
> Adsheartkins y'are all as errant Cullies.[8]

COMMENTARY: Behn's *The Rover*, the most popular of her plays, is a swashbuckling Restoration comedy set far from the drawing-rooms of London society. Its morality is loose and effervescent and its characters have a freedom of mind and movement which allows them to get involved in the most complex of arrangements and affairs. The plot of the play revolves around love affairs and disguises and owes a good deal to Shakespeare's romantic comedies, such as *As You Like It*. Behn's male and female characters are equal in their playfulness, independence and sexual confidence. They are deft matches for one another, and spend a good deal of the action working out elaborate tricks and deceptions.

Blunt, as his name implies, is a rough cut country 'gentleman'; not a gentleman in the way we understand that term today. You can hear in his voice a thick unrefined accent that is quick to seize consonants and the sounds they produce ('coxcomb', 'Quean', 'cozen'd', 'Essex Calf', etc.). He spouts all these words as though they were rich profanities. Blunt has literally just stepped out of deep shit, and as he speaks he is reeking both with indignity and the smell. He must also be incensed by the embarrassment and shame that are a result of his stupidity. In his haste to escape he left everything behind including his clothes so he is delivering the speech in his underwear, addressed to the audience. One imagines that he is literally trying to kick himself for his stupidity. His comic fury knows no bounds.

[7] **lousy** obscene
[8] **Cullies** deceived fools

The Double Dealer
(1694) William Congreve

Act 2, scene 1. London. A gallery in Lord Touchwood's house.

Maskwell (20s–30s), 'a villain and a gallant', is a pretended friend to the more virtuous Mellefont. They are both rivals for Cynthia although Maskwell hides that fact from Mellefont and pretends to act on his behalf as a go-between. After Mellefont leaves the stage, Maskwell reveals his real purpose and begins a plot to win Cynthia and her fortune for himself.

MASKWELL.
Till then, success will attend me; for when I meet you, I meet the only obstacle to my fortune. – Cynthia, let thy beauty gild my crimes; and whatsoever I commit of treachery or deceit, shall be imputed to me as a merit. – Treachery! what treachery? love cancels all the bonds of friendship, and sets men right upon their first foundations. – Duty to kings, piety to parents, gratitude to benefactors, and fidelity to friends, are different and particular ties: but the name of rival cuts 'em all asunder, and is a general acquittance. Rival is equal, and love like death, a universal leveller of mankind. Ha! but is there not such a thing as honesty? Yes, and whosoever has it about him bears an enemy in his breast: for your honest man, as I take it, is that nice scrupulous conscientious person, who will cheat nobody but himself: such another coxcomb as your wise man, who is too hard for all the world, and will be made a fool of by nobody but himself: ha! ha! ha! well, for wisdom and honesty, give me cunning and hypocrisy; oh, 'tis such a pleasure to angle for fair-faced fools! Then that hungry

gudgeon¹ credulity will bite at anything. – Why, let me see,
I have the same face, the same words and accents, when I
speak what I do think, and when I speak what I do not
think – the very same – and dear dissimulation is the only
art not to be known from nature.

Why will mankind be fools, and be deceived?
And why are friends and lovers' oaths believed?
When each who searches strictly his own mind,
May so much fraud and power of baseness find.

COMMENTARY: Congreve's *The Double Dealer*, like all of his
plays, is an incisive dissection of a society where falsehood or
double dealing is used as a manipulative device. The action of the
play is restricted to three hours after a dinner party on the eve
before Mellefont, nephew and prospective heir to Lord Touchwood, is about to marry Cynthia, the daughter of Sir Paul Plyant.
The devious and overtly promiscuous Lady Touchwood, herself
in love with Mellefont and rejected by him, enlists the aid of
Maskwell, the 'Double Dealer' and her former lover, to destroy
the relationship between Mellefont and Cynthia while the house is
full of all parties. Intrigue follows intrigue as the comic villains
up-end themselves in the final act.

Maskwell masks well his duplicitous nature, only revealing
himself in soliloquies like this one. He is a superb master of
cunning, a rogue who will stoop to anything to outflank Mellefont
and win Cynthia. His weapon is hypocrisy and as he says he treats
dissimulation as a form of art. Like all artists he loves to talk
about his work, which he does here directly to the audience. The
actor has to show a good deal of attention to the choice and
specificity of words and phrases. Maskwell is laying out a
reasoned argument and treats it like a lecture. If he muffs one
word or line the whole edifice will collapse so you have got to do
this obeying all the order and balance called for in the lines.
Notice the internal rhythms in the speech: 'for wisdom and
honesty give me cunning and hypocrisy'. You are guided through
the monologue by means of a hidden poetry and the speech works

¹ **gudgeon** a small bait fish often signifying someone easily fooled

best when you fall into the flow of its rhythm. The final quatrain is delivered as two rhyming couplets. After you have concentrated on those a bit see if you can use them to help trip your way through the longer bits. Notice too that the speech is full of polysyllabic words which are easy to bungle unless you see them as part of an overall pattern in which words are relished and brandished as the necessary tools of the double dealer: they are his trump cards.

Love for Love
(1695) William Congreve

Act 3, scene 3. London. A room in Foresight's house.

Tattle (30s), 'a half-witted Beau, vain of his amours, yet valuing himself for secrecy . . . is a public professor of secrecy, and makes proclamation that he holds private intelligence.' When asked to produce witnesses for his self-proclaimed indiscretions he retorts with the following defence.

TATTLE.

No? I can show letters, lockets, pictures, and rings; and if there be occasion for witnesses, I can summon the maids at the chocolate-houses, all the porters at Pall-Mall and Covent-Garden, the door-keepers at the play-house, the drawers at Locket's, Pontac's, the Rummer, Spring-Garden;[1] my own landlady, and valet-de-chambre; all who shall make oath, that I receive more letters than the Secretary's Office, and that I have more vizor-masks[2] to inquire for me than ever went to see the Hermaphrodite, or the Naked Prince.[3] And it is notorious, that in a country church, once, an inquiry being made who I was, it was answered, I was the famous Tattle, who had ruined so many women . . . True. I was called Turk-Tattle all over the parish. – The next Sunday all the old women kept their daughters at home, and the parson had not half his congregation. He would have brought me into the spiritual court, but I was revenged upon him, for he had a handsome

[1] **Locket's . . . Spring-Garden** all noted taverns and pleasure gardens
[2] **vizor-masks** prostitutes
[3] **Hermaphrodite / Naked Prince** popular sideshow attractions in London

84

daughter, whom I initiated into the science. But I repented it afterwards, for it was talked of in town; and a lady of quality, that shall be nameless, in a raging fit of jealousy, came down in her coach and six horses, and exposed herself upon my account; gad, I was sorry for it with all my heart. – You know whom I mean – you know where we raffled[4] – . . . Gad so, the heat of my story carried me beyond my discretion, as the heat of the lady's passion hurried her beyond her reputation. – But I hope you don't know whom I mean; for there a great many ladies raffled. – Pox on't! now could I bite off my tongue. . . . For Heaven's sake if you do guess, say nothing; gad, I'm very unfortunate.

COMMENTARY: Congreve's *Love for Love* has a fast-paced plot that covers a wide range of absurd characters and situations. It deals with an interlocking series of comic plots in which intrigue, inheritance, romance, scandal, astrology, deceit and wit are all part of the comic web. The genuine delight in the play is the wealth of characters with each one carefully drawn and speaking his or her very own language.

Tattle is a superb example of the kind of character who fills the action of the play. He is a foppish man about town who carries the weight and opinion of London wherever he goes. In this speech he attempts to substantiate his importance as a gossip and town chronicler and goes into exaggerated details about the places and people he knows and about his prowess in destroying reputations. Tattle is also a born playwright who can create scenes and other characters with such relish that his listeners swear they have met them in the flesh. He peppers his tale with such passionate engagement that he tends to lose the thread and is always on the verge of naming names and compromising important ladies. The actor has to draw in his listeners with his titillating tattle.

[4] **raffled** an unclear reference but the actor can speculate on its meaning

The Relapse
(1696) Sir John Vanbrugh

Act 2, scene 1. London. A drawing-room.

Lord Foppington (30s) is 'a vain coxcomb' proud of his newly purchased lordship which has only been in effect for forty-eight hours. Previously known as Sir Novelty Fashion, he hopes his new title will secure him a wealthy heiress as a wife. Here he is paying his respects to Amanda and Loveless, telling his captive audience about his life as a man of mode.

LORD FOPPINGTON.

. . . Far example, Madam, my life: my life, Madam, is a perpetual stream of pleasure, that glides through such a variety of entertainments, I believe the wisest of our ancestors never had the least conception of any of 'em. I rise, Madam, about ten a-clack. I don't rise sooner, because 'tis the worst thing in the world for the complexion; nat that I pretend to be a beau: but a man must endeavour to look wholesome, lest he make so nauseous a figure in the side-bax,[1] the ladies should be compelled to turn their eyes upon the play. So at ten a-clack I say I rise. Naw if I find 'tis a good day, I resalve to take a turn in the Park, and see the fine women: so huddle on[2] my clothes, and get dressed by one. If it be nasty weather, I take a turn in the chocolate-hause; where, as you walk Madam, you have the prettiest prospect in the world; you have looking-glasses all round you. – But I'm afraid I tire the company?

[BERINTHIA. Not at all. Pray go on.]

[1] **side-bax** i.e. a side-box at a playhouse
[2] **huddle on** hastily put on

Why then, ladies, from thence I go to dinner at Lacket's;[3] where you are so nicely and delicately served, that, stap my vitals, they shall compose you a dish no bigger than a saucer, shall come to fifty shillings. Between eating my dinner, (and washing my mauth, ladies) I spend my time, 'till I go to the play;[4] where, 'till nine a-clack, I entertain myself with looking upon the company; and usually dispose of one hour more in leading 'em aut. So there's twelve of the four and twenty pretty well over. The other twelve, Madam, are disposed of in two articles: in the first four, I toast myself drunk, and in t'other eight, I sleep myself sober again. Thus ladies you see my life is an eternal raund O of delights.

COMMENTARY: Vanbrugh's *The Relapse, or Virtue in Danger* is a comedy that follows the fall from virtue of the character Loveless with his wife's cousin Berinthia, while his wife Amanda is being chased by Worthy, a gentleman of the town. All is righted in the end and virtue triumphs. In the sub-plot Young Fashion schemes to cheat his older brother Lord Foppington out of his intended bride, Miss Hoyden, a naïve country heiress who is the daughter of Sir Tunbelly Clumsy. The play is a comic delight largely because of the rich characterisations.

Lord Foppington is a city fop in the tradition of Sir Fopling Flutter, a character in Sir George Etherege's *The Man of Mode*. Whenever he is on stage he tends to dominate the action. Notice here how he dominates the dialogue. He is vain and egotistical and his whole life is devoted to pleasure and using up the hours of the day in pursuit of it. He speaks in an affected manner stressing vowels in the most sharply peculiar way and elongating words wherever he can for emphasis. This is how he thinks the nobility talks. Words to him are like fashionable clothes that he puts on. He is full of self-importance and eager to show off his newly purchased title, and like any man about town he defines himself to strangers largely through name-dropping and mentioning

[3] **Lacket's** a famous tavern near Charing Cross
[4] **the play** plays generally began before six p.m.

fashionable 'in' spots. He is a character, no doubt, with as many physical quirks as verbal ones. The actor has to think about how to perform Lord Foppington: how does he look and move? The character is already exaggerated enough and needs no further help in this direction. So play him as a vain coxcomb who seems barely aware that he is boring his company to death with the minutiae of his daily life. In showing off he is trying to show how he fits in. That is a positive aspect of all his posturing and one which saves him from being totally ridiculous.

The Provok'd Wife
(1697) Sir John Vanbrugh

Act 1, scene 1. London. Sir John Brute's house.

Sir John Brute (30s–40s), brutish and boorish, opens the play with this soliloquy full of complaints about marriage.

SIR JOHN:
What cloying[1] meat is love, – when matrimony's the sauce
to it. Two years' marriage has debauched my five senses.
Everything I see, everything I hear, everything I feel,
everything I smell, and everything I taste – methinks has
wife in't. No boy was ever so weary of his tutor; no girl of
her bib; no nun of doing penance nor old maid of being
chaste, as I am of being married. Sure there's a secret curse
entailed upon the very name of wife. My lady is a young
lady, a fine lady, a witty lady, a virtuous lady – and yet I
hate her. There is but one thing on earth I loathe beyond
her: that's fighting. Would my courage come up but to a
fourth part of my ill nature, I'd stand buff[2] to her relations,
and thrust her out of doors. But marriage has sunk me
down to such an ebb of resolution, I dare not draw my
sword, though even to get rid of my wife. But here she
comes.

COMMENTARY: Vanbrugh's *The Provok'd Wife* revolves around
the unsatisfactory marriage of Sir John and Lady Brute which must
continue because a divorce is not possible. The institution of
marriage becomes a ripe comic target in the form of various

[1] **cloying** nauseating
[2] **buff** firm

adulterous liaisons. Lady Brute encourages the attentions of her admirer Constant and becomes involved in a series of compromising affairs which lead to nothing in the end. A host of romantic sub-plots keeps the action on the level of farce.

Sir John Brute is as gruff and unpleasant as his name implies. Not the sort of man who should ever get married, but precisely the sort of man whose stiff and uncompromising manner make him an apt target for comic puncturing. His soliloquy, though short, is wonderfully speakable. It revolves around the senses and what marriage has done to alter them. Notice how he uses simple and direct words ('hate', 'buff', 'thrust', 'sunk', 'ebb', 'rid') to signal his displeasure; he practically grunts them. Unlike the fops in eighteenth-century drama, John Brute is a refreshing antidote largely because he is so brief and concise when he speaks.

The Constant Couple
(1699) George Farquhar

Act 5, scene 1. London. A room in Lady Darling's house.

Sir Harry Wildair (20s), 'an airy gentleman, affecting humorous gaiety and freedom in his behaviour', arrives at Lady Darling's house drunk and in pursuit of the virtuous Angelica. He has been deceived by his rival Vizard, who is resentful of his interest in Lady Lurewell, into believing that Angelica is in fact a prostitute and her mother is her bawd. In his drunken state he tries to negotiate a suitable fee to procure Angelica's 'virtue'.

SIR HARRY WILDAIR (*aside*).
This is the first whore in heroics that I have met with. (*Aloud.*) Look ye, madam, as to that slander particular of your virtue, we sha'n't quarrel about it; you may be as virtuous as any woman in England, if you please; you may say your prayers all the time. – But pray, madam, be pleased to consider what is this same virtue that you make such a mighty noise about? Can your virtue bespeak you a front row in the boxes?[1] No; for the players can't live upon virtue. Can your virtue keep you a coach and six? No, no, your virtuous women walk a-foot. Can your virtue hire you a pew in a church? Why, the very sexton will tell you, no. Can your virtue stake for you at picquet?[2] No. Then what business has a woman with virtue? Come, come, madam, I offered you fifty guineas: there's a hundred. – The devil! Virtuous still! Why, 'tis a hundred, five score, a hundred guineas. . . . Affront! 'Sdeath, madam! a hundred guineas will set you up at basset,[3] a hundred guineas will furnish

[1] **boxes** i.e. boxes at the theatre
[2] **piquet** a card game for two players
[3] **basset** a Venetian card game

out your lodgings with china; a hundred guineas will give you an air of quality; a hundred guineas will buy you a rich escritoir[4] for your billets-doux,[5] or a fine Common-Prayer-Book for your virtue. A hundred guineas will buy a hundred fine things, and fine things are for fine ladies; and fine ladies are for fine gentlemen; and fine gentlemen are – egad, this burgundy makes a man speak like an angel. – Come, come, madam, take it and put it to what use you please.

COMMENTARY: Farquhar's *The Constant Couple* is one of the most unbridled comedies of the Restoration period. The plot revolves around a series of sexual intrigues. Lady Lurewell is determined to be revenged upon all the male sex and her victims include the free-spirited Sir Harry Wildair plus Smuggler, Vizard, Clincher and Colonel Standard. Hypocrisy is a mask that hides lewd and avaricious intentions and even the virtuous Angelica is made to seem a whore. After all the mayhem of mistaken intentions and identities evil is unmasked, virtue conquers all and the 'constant couple' united in love.

Sir Harry Wildair's speech is as robust and hearty as the burgundy that fuels it. As their names imply, Wildair and Angelica in this encounter become beast and angel to one another. The monologue contains a minefield of words that can be easily slurred by a drunken tongue so the actor has to work extra hard to articulate the sentences while physicalising the drunkenness and staying steady on his feet. Do not focus on his drunkenness but play a man who thinks he is sober although his tongue keeps giving him away. Remember he thinks he is 'speaking like an angel'. His references are very specific to all the aspects of fashionable city life and what 'virtue' can and cannot 'purchase'. Harry has just been throwing money around the stage and much of this speech is about wagering. As Harry's frustration grows he recklessly increases his bid for Angelica's 'virtue' until he gets to a hundred guineas (equivalent to about £60,000 today). Notice how he tries to force his point by a series of rhetorical questions and answers. These are a gift for the actor to play with.

[4] **escritoir** a writing desk
[5] **billets-doux** love letters

The Way of the World
(1700) William Congreve

Act 4, scene 1. London. A room in Lady Wishfort's house.

Edward Mirabell (20s–30s) is a fine society gentleman. He is rakish, calculating, witty and thoroughly schooled in 'the way of the world'. Throughout the play he pursues and woos Mrs¹ Millamant. In this scene Mrs Millamant has just revealed the conditions under which she will contemplate and tolerate his proposal of marriage. This speech is his retort.

MIRABELL.
Your bill of fare is something advanced in this latter account. – Well, have I liberty to offer conditions – that when you are dwindled into a wife, I may not be beyond measure enlarged into a husband? . . . I thank you. – *Imprimis²* then, I covenant, that your acquaintance be general; that you admit no sworn confidant, or intimate of your own sex; no she friend to screen her affairs under your countenance, and tempt you to make trial of a mutual secrecy. No decoy duck to wheedle you a fop-scrambling to the play in a mask³ – then bring you home in a pretended fright, when you think you shall be found out – and rail⁴ at me for missing the play, and disappointing the frolic which you had to pick me up, and prove my constancy. . . . *Item*, I article, that you continue to like your own face, as long as I shall: and while it passes current with me, that you

¹ **Mrs** in Congreve's time the designation Mrs was used for both married and unmarried women
² **Imprimis** In the first place (the phrase is used in legal documents)
³ **mask** playgoers would often attend theatres wearing masks
⁴ **rail** complain

endeavour not to new-coin it. To which end, together with all vizards[5] for the day, I prohibit all masks for the night, made of oiled-skins, and I know not what – hogs' bones, hares' gall, pig-water, and the marrow of a roasted cat. In short, I forbid all commerce with the gentlewomen of what d'ye call it court. *Item*, I shut my doors against all bawds with baskets, and pennyworths of muslin, china, fans, atlases,[6] etc. *Item*, when you shall be breeding – . . . Which may be presumed with a blessing on our endeavours. . . . I denounce against all strait lacing, squeezing for a shape, till you mould my boy's head like a sugar-loaf, and instead of a man child, make me father to a crooked billet.[7] Lastly, to the dominion of the tea-table I submit – but with proviso, that you exceed not in your province; but restrain yourself to native and simple tea-table drinks, as tea, chocolate, and coffee; as likewise to genuine and authorised tea-table talk – such as mending of fashions, spoiling reputations, railing at absent friends, and so forth – but that on no account you encroach upon the men's prerogative, and presume to drink healths, or toast fellows; for prevention of which I banish all foreign forces, all auxiliaries to the tea-table, as orange-brandy, all aniseed, cinnamon, citron, and Barbadoes water, together with ratafia, and the most noble spirit of clary – but for cowslip wine, poppy water, and dormitives,[8] those I allow. – These provisos admitted, in other things I may prove a tractable and complying husband.

COMMENTARY: The intricate plot of *The Way of the World* partly revolves around the attempts of the urbane and witty Mirabell to marry the equally sophisticated and quick-witted

[5] **vizards** masks
[6] **atlases** satins
[7] **billet** thick stick of wood
[8] **orange-brandy . . . dormitives** various kinds of alcoholic and non-alcoholic beverages

Millamant. Their world is the insulated one of stylish high society with a strict set of codes and manners. Property and keeping property are a central concern. Characters use language in an ironic and complex way both as an offensive and defensive weapon that maps out the ownership of space and keeps emotion under wraps. Congreve's play is full of brilliant scenes, sparkling dialogue and lifelike characterisations. It should be acted as realistically as possible without any affected or caricatured mannerisms whatsoever. The dialogue should feel contemporary and not antique.

Act Four of the drama contains the famous 'bargaining' scene in which Millamant and Mirabell agree to marry after negotiating an intricate verbal contract setting forth the various rights and responsibilities of one towards the other. The language of this monologue must be performed with these legalistic intentions in mind. Notice that this is not a speech about love. At no point does he declare himself or reveal his affections for Millamant. In other words this is not a romantic speech but contains provisos and warnings. Note, for instance, how he itemises and lists the things that she can and cannot do as his wife. Millamant has just set out her conditions like a lawyer dictating terms and Mirabell tops her with an even lengthier catalogue of conditions which he in his turn will impose on her. The wit and fun in the speech are contained in the elaborately articulated lists, words and exotic references that verge on the fantastical. The actor should play an intelligent man who knows his opponent well, and not just act the fop.

The Rivals
(1775) Richard Brinsley Sheridan

Act 3, scene 2. Bath. Julia's dressing-room.

Faulkland (20s) is in love with Julia Melville. He has been pressing her to define the nature of her love for him but she becomes worn down by his constant badgering and suspicion and runs out of the room in tears.

FAULKLAND.
In tears! stay Julia, stay but for a moment. – The door is fastened! – Julia! – my soul – but for one moment – I hear her sobbing! 'Sdeath! what a brute am I to use her thus! Yet stay – aye – she is coming now: how little resolution there is in woman! – how a few soft words can turn them! No, faith! – she is *not* coming either. Why, Julia – my love – say but that you forgive me – come but to tell me that – now, this is being *too* resentful: stay! she *is* coming too – I thought she would – no steadiness in anything! Her going away must have been a mere trick then – she shan't see that I was hurt by it. I'll affect indifference – (*Hums a tune; then listens.*) – no – zounds! she's *not* coming! – nor don't intend it, I suppose. This is not steadiness, but obstinacy! Yet I deserve it. What, after so long an absence, to quarrel with her tenderness! – 'twas barbarous and unmanly! I should be ashamed to see her now. I'll wait till her just resentment is abated – and when I distress her so again, may I lose her for ever! and be linked instead to some antique virago,[1] whose gnawing passions, and long-hoarded spleen, shall make me curse my folly half the day and all the night!

[1] **virago** quarrelsome woman

COMMENTARY: Sheridan's *The Rivals* is a comedy of intrigue and mistaken identity. Sir Anthony Absolute wants his son Captain Absolute to marry the wealthy heiress Lydia Languish. He is unaware that Captain Absolute is already wooing Lydia disguised as the dashing Ensign Beverley, a role he has adopted to fulfil Lydia's romantic notions of elopement. Lydia's aunt Mrs Malaprop disapproves of the poor Beverley and threatens to disinherit Lydia if she marries him rather than Captain Absolute. A second sub-plot involves the sentimental pair of lovers Faulkland and Julia Melville. All is straightened out in the end after much complication, farce, and comic anguish.

Faulkland is the epitome of the sentimental hero carried to extremes. Excessively romantic, his attachment to his love makes him hear and see things which are not there. As he says earlier in the play, 'I think I love beyond my life, I am ever ungenerously fretful, and madly capricious! I am conscious of it – yet I cannot correct myself!' So Faulkland is a prisoner of love and a captive to his fixation on Julia. Notice how he speaks almost entirely in exclamations. There is a heightened theatricality in his manner of delivery. No matter what anyone says to him, Faulkland will always act the role of the disappointed lover. The speech also demands a great deal of physical acting. Faulkland is speaking to a door in desperate anticipation of Julia's return and has to use it as a prop to touch and listen at. The timing of movement in relation to the lines becomes very important. He sets himself up to be rejected and disappointed so the shut door is the perfect obstacle for him to act against. In a single speech he goes through a rainbow of emotions. Like all of the characters in the play he is consumed by one absolute state of mind.

The Critic

(1779) Richard Brinsley Sheridan

Act 1, scene 2. London. The drawing-room of Mr and Mrs Dangle.

Mr Puff (40s), an author and literary entrepreneur, has come to visit Mr Dangle, a hack theatre critic. In this scene he is telling Dangle and his friend Sneer his life 'history' and the hardships he has conquered.

PUFF.
And, in truth, I deserved what I got; for I suppose never man went through such a series of calamities in the same space of time! Sir, I was five times made a bankrupt, and reduced from a state of affluence by a train of unavoidable misfortunes! Then, sir, through a very industrious trades-man, I was twice burnt out, and lost my little all, both times! I lived upon those fires a month. I soon after was confined by a most excruciating disorder, and lost the use of my limbs! That told very well; for I had the case strongly attested, and went about to collect the subscriptions myself.

[DANGLE. Egad, I believe that was when you first called on me –]

In November last? Oh, no! – I was at that time a close prisoner in the Marshalsea,[1] for a debt benevolently con-tracted to serve a friend! I was afterwards twice tapped for a dropsy, which declined into a very profitable consumption! I was then reduced to – oh, no, then, I became a widow with six helpless children – after having had eleven hus-bands pressed, and being left every time eight months gone with child, and without money to get me into a hospital!

[1] **Marshalsea** a notorious debtor's prison in south London

[SNEER. And you bore all with patience, I make no doubt?]

Why, yes, though I made some occasional attempts at *felo de se*;[2] but as I did not find those *rash actions* answer, I left off killing myself very soon. Well, sir, at last what with bankruptcies, fires, gouts, dropsies, imprisonments, and other valuable calamities, having got together a pretty handsome sum, I determined to quit a business which had always gone rather against my conscience, and in a more liberal ways till to indulge my talents for fiction and embellishment, through my favourite channels of diurnal communication – and so, sir, you have my history.

COMMENTARY: Sheridan's *The Critic, or A Tragedy Rehearsed* is a burlesque comedy based on Buckingham's play *The Rehearsal*. The hilarious action focuses on the problems of producing a ludicrous tragic drama called *The Spanish Armada*. The play is written by the enterprising Mr Puff who involves two hack critics in the process of the play's rehearsal which moves by fits and interruptions to a conclusion resembling a Marx Brothers film.

Mr Puff, as his name implies, is all puff and bluster. As he says earlier 'I love to . . . advertise myself *viva voce*[3] I am, sir, a practitioner in panegyric, or to speak more plainly – a professor of the art of puffing.' Notice that his speech is full of tongue-twisting combinations of consonants. His life is a catalogue of disasters averted and equals the outrageous dramas he writes for the stage. Puff is also something of a con-man who preys on the sentimentality of his audience and as with any good con-man it is difficult for either Dangle or Sneer to get a word in edgeways. He fills up all the gaps with tale after tale of tragic woe, but note how he has turned each of these to his financial benefit: Mr Puff delights in insurance scams and financial chicanery of all sorts. Puff is a chameleon-like character who can shift mood, profession and personality as expediency dictates. At one point he transforms

[2] **felo de se** suicide
[3] **viva voce** orally

into a widow with six helpless children and eleven previous husbands! There is so much that he is bursting to convey that he speaks almost entirely in run-on sentences. He is all hyperbole and exaggeration and the actor should throw himself into the character with a full appetite for both.

Lady Windermere's Fan
(1892) Oscar Wilde

Act 2. London. Drawing-room of Lord Windermere's house in Carlton House Terrace.

Lord Darlington (30s–40s), an elegant, witty bachelor, is attending Lady Windermere's ball celebrating her 'coming of age'. He is planning to leave England and this is his last chance to declare his true feelings to Lady Windermere. He is trying to steal her away from her husband and does so by confirming the rumour that Lord Windermere is having an affair with Mrs Erlynne who is also attending the party. Lady Windermere seeks his advice and comfort as a 'friend' and he decides to seize his opportunity.

LORD DARLINGTON.
If I know you at all, I know that you can't live with a man who treats you like this! What sort of a life would you have with him? You would feel that he was lying to you every moment of the day. You would feel that the look in his eyes was false, his voice false, his touch false, his passion false. He would come to you when he was weary of others; you would have to comfort him. He would come to you when he was devoted to others; you would have to charm him. You would have to be to him the mask of his real life, the cloak to hide his secret. . . . Between men and women there is no friendship possible. There is passion, enmity, worship, love, but no friendship. I love you – . . . Yes, I love you! You are more to me than anything in the world. What does your husband give you? Nothing. Whatever is in him he gives to this wretched woman, who he has thrust into your society, into your home, to shame you before everyone. I offer you my life – . . . My life – my whole life. Take it, and do with it what you will. . . . I love you – love you as I have

never loved any living thing. From the moment I met you I loved you, loved you blindly, adoringly, madly! You did not know it then – you know it now! Leave this house tonight. I won't tell you that the world matters nothing, or the world's voice, or the voice of society. They matter a great deal. They matter far too much. But there are moments when one has to choose between living one's own life, fully, entirely, completely – or dragging out some false, shallow, degrading existence that the world in its hypocrisy demands. You have that moment now. Choose! Oh, my love, choose.

COMMENTARY: Wilde's *Lady Windermere's Fan* is a comedy of manners that pits romance against intrigue. A dropped fan becomes the crucial piece of evidence in this 'well-made play'. Hurt and upset that her husband is showing interest in Mrs Erlynne, a woman of doubtful reputation, Lady Windermere decides to leave him and run off with Lord Darlington, a persistent and charming suitor. Mrs Erlynne, actually Lady Windermere's mother, deserted her husband and daughter many years earlier, before being deserted herself. She learns of Lady Windermere's rash decision – by means of a dropped note meant for Lord Windermere – and rushes to Lord Darlington's rooms. Here the main complications of the plot ensue as Mrs Erlynne works to protect Lady Windermere's reputation by claiming that Lady Windermere's incriminating fan, found in Lord Darlington's rooms, is one she had picked up at Lady Windermere's ball, casting further doubt on her own integrity. Vital reputation is preserved and the intrigue works to produce a happy conclusion.

Lord Darlington is a distant relative of the rakish rogues of eighteenth-century drama. He is described in the play as 'a charming, wicked creature'. He prowls the drawing-rooms of fashionable society looking for distressed ladies in need of his affections. Lady Windermere is just the kind of woman he is drawn to and he quickly sizes up a potentially adulterous situation in the hopes that he can turn it to his advantage. The proofs he offers Lady Windermere, though circumstantial, are supported by his earnest and robust declaration of love. Darlington seizes his opportunity and makes the most of it. The play is ruled by time (the action takes place within twenty-four hours) so the character must do his seducing quickly, in order to move the plot forwards to its next stage. But it is an elegantly patterned speech which must be delivered with a great deal of sincerity and ardour; two qualities quite alien to Lord Darlington. Notice how Wilde has written the speech to be spoken out loud with fervour. You can deliver chunks of phrases at a time; you are building an argument and assault and you marshal a full battery of eloquence to achieve it. The speech has a rapturous forward momentum.

A Woman of No Importance
(1893) Oscar Wilde

Act 3. The hall at Hunstanton Chase.

Gerald Arbuthnot (early 20s) is Mrs Arbuthnot's son, in love with Hester, a young, wealthy American visitor. He is extremely ambitious and eager to move up in the world and has been offered a position as a private secretary to Lord Illingworth: 'The world says that Lord Illingworth is very, very wicked.' His mother is very disconcerted that he is going away to work for Lord Illingworth.

[GERALD. . . . I have never been so happy.
MRS ARBUTHNOT. At the prospect of going away?]
GERALD.
Don't put it like that, mother. Of course I am sorry to leave you. Why, you are the best mother in the whole world. But after all, as Lord Illingworth says, it is impossible to live in such a place as Wrockley. You don't mind it. But I'm ambitious; I want something more than that. I want to have a career. I want to do something that will make you proud of me, and Lord Illingworth is going to help me. He is going to do everything for me. . . . Mother, how changeable you are! You don't seem to know your own mind for a single moment. An hour and a half ago in the Drawing-room you agreed to the whole thing; now you turn round and make objections, and try to force me to give up my one chance in life. Yes, my one chance. You don't suppose that men like Lord Illingworth are to be found every day, do you, mother? It is very strange that when I have had such a wonderful piece of good luck, the one person to put difficulties in my way should be my own mother. Besides, you know, mother, I love Hester Worsley. Who could help

loving her? I love her more than I have ever told you, far more. And if I had a position, if I had prospects, I could – I could ask her to – Don't you understand now, mother, what it means to me to be Lord Illingworth's secretary? To start like this is to find a career ready for one – before one – waiting for one. If I were Lord Illingworth's secretary I could ask Hester to be my wife. As a wretched bank clerk with a hundred a year it would be an impertinence. . . . Then I have my ambition left, at any rate. That is something – I am glad I have that! You have always tried to crush my ambition, mother – haven't you? You have told me that the world is a wicked place, that success is not worth having, that society is shallow, and all that sort of thing – well, I don't believe it, mother. I think the world must be delightful. I think society must be exquisite. I think success is a thing worth having. You have been wrong in all that you taught me, mother, quite wrong. Lord Illingworth is a successful man. He is a fashionable man. He is a man who lives in the world and for it. Well, I would give anything to be just like Lord Illingworth.

COMMENTARY: Wilde's *A Woman of No Importance*, although a comedy, deals with serious subjects: illegitimacy and the sexual exploitation of women. Set on a country estate it focuses on class and the role of outsiders in that society. A youthful romance between Rachel Arbuthnot and George Harford (later Lord Illingworth) produced a child, Gerald Arbuthnot. Illingworth, despite having promised to marry Rachel, ignominiously abandoned her, turning his back on her and the child he has never known. This leads to Gerald becoming totally dependent on his mother and ignorant of either his origins or his true relationship to Lord Illingworth, a man who now wants to employ him as his private secretary. Illingworth himself only finds out he is Gerald's father at the climactic end of Act Three. The sins of the past now surface in the present and must be reconciled. By the close of the play the Arbuthnots turn their back on Lord Illingworth, rejecting him, his money and everything he stands for.

Gerald requires a special kind of handling in performance. His youth and a life spent in the company of women give an emotional edge to his monologue. It is a melodramatic scene, but you have to guard against the inclination to give in to the melodrama. This is an assertive speech, not a surrender, so play the character's revolt and need for freedom and independence. Gerald's ambition surfaces in this scene: he wants to be a success, to be wealthy and in a position to marry the woman of his choice, Hester. He does not want to remain a bank clerk. For the first time in his life his horizons are widening and in Lord Illingworth he has found an appropriate man to emulate. The speech is pulling Gerald away from his mother, and the words should be used to distance you from her. He is making his bid for freedom and he intends to seize it.

The Second Mrs Tanqueray
(1893) Arthur Wing Pinero

Act 1. London. Aubrey Tanqueray's Chambers in the Albany.

Cayley Drummle is a man about town who stops by Tanqueray's apartment for after-dinner drinks. In Pinero's description he is 'a neat little man of about five-and-forty, in manner bright, airy, debonair, but with an undercurrent of seriousness.'

DRUMMLE.
It so happens that to-night I was exceptionally *early* in dressing for dinner. . . . At a quarter to eight, in fact, I found myself trimming my nails, with ten minutes to spare. Just then enter my man with a note – would I hasten, as fast as cab could carry me, to old Lady Orreyed in Bruton Street? – 'sad trouble'. Now recollect, please, I had ten minutes on my hands, old Lady Orreyed was a very dear friend of my mother's, and was in some distress . . . (*With mock indignation.*) Upon my word! Well, the scene in Bruton Street beggars description; the women servants looked scared, the men drunk; and there was poor old Lady Orreyed on the floor of her boudoir like Queen Bess among her pillows. . . . (*To everyone.*) You know George Orreyed? . . . Well, he's a thing of the past . . . He's married Mabel Hervey . . . It's true – this morning. The poor mother showed me his letter – a dozen curt words, and some of them ill-spelt . . . (*He sits.*) Miss Hervey – Lady Orreyed, as she now is – was a lady who would have been, perhaps had been described in the reports of the Police or the Divorce Court as an actress. Had she belonged to a lower stratum of our advanced civilisation she would, in the event of judicial inquiry, have defined her calling with equal

justification as that of a dressmaker. To do her justice, she is a type of a class which is immortal. Physically, by the strange caprice of creation, curiously beautiful; mentally, she lacks even the strength of deliberate viciousness. (*He rises and moves centre.*) Paint her portrait, it would symbolise a creature perfectly patrician; lance a vein of her superbly-modelled arm, you would get poorest *vin ordinaire*! Her affections, emotions, impulses, her very existence – a burlesque! Flaxen, five-and-twenty, and feebly frolicsome; anybody's, in less gentle society I should say everybody's, property! That, Doctor, was Miss Hervey who is the new Lady Orreyed. Dost thou like the picture?

COMMENTARY: Pinero's *The Second Mrs Tanqueray* is a classic problem play, set in the world of high society, which has a woefully unhappy ending. Paula, the heroine, is a woman with a questionable past. She marries the older, widowed Aubrey Tanqueray and retires with him to his country home, but is not accepted by his friends or by his nineteen-year-old daughter Ellean. The arrival of Ellean's suitor, one of Paula's former lovers, provokes a series of disastrous revelations and strife. The play ends with Paula's suicide.

Cayley Drummle is a social gadabout whose brief appearance gives us an amusing picture of life behind the façades of the elegant houses of Mayfair. This is a world in which former actresses (considered to be disreputable women) can marry well with nobles or gentlemen of property. His diverting story paints a slice-of-life scene of high drama with farcical overtones. Drummle is something of a melodramatist, keeping his audience enthralled with climax after climax and teasing questions. The women are vividly portrayed in his tale. An actor should remember that Pinero loved to create lots of details which give the performer something on which to concentrate his imagination, i.e. 'I found myself trimming my nails with ten minutes to spare . . .' So you can move through this speech step by step until you have created an elaborately embroidered picture of people and a social world. Pinero was also insistent that his actor move with the speech as it shifts attention, to protect him from becoming boring: notice his indications of this in the stage directions. He wanted the actor to fill the stage with his story-telling presence.

An Ideal Husband
(1895) Oscar Wilde

Act 2. London. Morning-room in Sir Robert Chiltern's house.

Sir Robert Chiltern (40), a Member of Parliament and a Cabinet Under-Secretary, is being blackmailed for having sold secret government documents twenty years prior to the beginning of the action. Here he has just been confronted by his wife Lady Gertrude Chiltern who is shattered by the revelation of his crime. She had believed him to be the ideal husband, 'the ideal, as she says, of my life!' He immediately replies.

SIR ROBERT CHILTERN.

There was your mistake. There was your error. The error all women commit. Why can't you women love us, faults and all? Why do you place us on monstrous pedestals? We have all feet of clay, women as well as men; but when we men love women, we love them knowing their weaknesses, their follies, their imperfections, love them all the more, it may be, for that reason. It is not the perfect, but the imperfect, who have need of love. It is when we are wounded by our own hands, or by the hands of others, that Love should come to cure us – else what use is love at all? All sins, except a sin against itself, Love should forgive. All lives, save loveless lives, true Love should pardon. A man's love is like that. It is wider, larger, more human than a woman's. Women think that they are making ideals of men. What they are making of us are false idols merely. You made your false idol of me, and I had not the courage to come down, show you my wounds, tell you my weaknesses. I was afraid that I might lose your love, as I have lost it now. And so, last night you ruined my life for me – yes, ruined it!

What this woman asked of me was nothing compared to what she offered to me. She offered security, peace, stability. The sin of my youth, that I had thought was buried, rose up in front of me, hideous, horrible, with its hands at my throat. I could have killed it for ever, sent it back into its tomb, destroyed its record, burned the one witness against me. You prevented me. No one but you, you know it. And now what is there before me but public disgrace, ruin, terrible shame, the mockery of the world, a lonely dishonoured life, a lonely dishonoured death, it may be, some day? Let women make no more ideals of men! let them not put them on altars and bow before them, or they may ruin other lives as completely as you – you whom I have so wildly loved – have ruined mine! (*He passes from the room.*)

COMMENTARY: Wilde's *An Ideal Husband* is an ironic comedy that attacks the notion of an 'ideal' anyone. Twenty years before the start of the play, the well-regarded and morally upstanding Sir Robert Chiltern, currently an Under-Secretary for Foreign Affairs, sold classified government secrets to the unscrupulous Baron Arnheim to secure his future position and fortune. The action of the play focuses on his blackmail by Mrs Cheveley, a former lover of the Baron, who is trying to gain government influence for a project in which she is investing. The moral quandary is revealed to Sir Robert's wife Lady Gertrude Chiltern and domestic strife is the result. Love corrects the balance in the end and reputations are only bruised.

Robert Chiltern is seen by Wilde as a striking character. Here is how he describes him: 'A man of forty, but looking somewhat younger. Clean-shaven, with finely-cut features, dark-haired and dark-eyed. A personality of mark. Not popular – few personalities are. But intensely admired by the few, and deeply respected by the many. The note of his manner is that of perfect distinction, with a slight touch of pride. One feels that he is conscious of the success he has made in life. A nervous temperament with a tired look . . .' His speech is an antidote to his wife's embracement of a high moral position which she thinks so-called 'men of honour' should embody. Chiltern knows that human beings are fallible and imperfect. The actor should play this as a realistic speech and not at all melodramatically. It is also a chance for the character finally to come to terms with a guilt he has been hiding for years. Use the flood of words as if they are an atonement motivated by the gravity of his situation. The actor should remember that this speech closes the second act of the play, so it must be delivered with concentrated authority.

Man and Superman
(1903) Bernard Shaw

Act 1. London. Roebuck Ramsden's handsome study.

John Tanner (30s–40s), a proud and brilliant man, engages in a debate with young Octavius (Tavy) Robinson about all manner of philosophical opinions and subjects, including women and the purpose of the artist. Tanner launches into a monologue about where the artist fits within the domestic scheme.

TANNER.
. . . The true artist will let his wife starve, his children go barefoot, his mother drudge for his living at seventy, sooner than work at anything but his art. To women he is half vivisector, half vampire. He gets into intimate relations with them to study them, to strip the mask of convention from them, to surprise their inmost secrets, knowing that they have the power to rouse his deepest creative energies, to rescue him from his cold reason, to make him see visions and dream dreams, to inspire him, as he calls it. He persuades women that they may do this for their own purpose whilst he really means them to do it for his. He steals the mother's milk and blackens it to make printer's ink to scoff at her and glorify ideal women with. He pretends to spare her the pangs of child-bearing so that he may have for himself the tenderness and fostering that belong of right to her children. Since marriage began, the great artist has been known as a bad husband. But he is worse: he is a child-robber, a blood-sucker, a hypocrite, and a cheat. Perish the race and wither a thousand women if only the sacrifice of them enable him to act Hamlet better, to paint a finer picture, to write a deeper poem, a greater

play, a profounder philosophy! For mark you, Tavy, the artist's work is to shew us ourselves as we really are. Our minds are nothing but this knowledge of ourselves; and he who adds a jot to such knowledge creates new minds as surely as any woman creates new men. In the rage of that creation he is as ruthless as the woman, as dangerous to her as she to him, and as horribly fascinating. Of all human struggles there is none so treacherous and remorseless as the struggle between the artist man and the mother woman. Which shall use up the other? that is the issue between them. And it is all the deadlier because, in your romanticist cant, they love one another.

COMMENTARY: Shaw's *Man and Superman*, subtitled 'A Comedy and a Philosophy', is a play about the eternal pursuit of the male by the female. It takes many detours into a variety of philosophical fields and shows Shaw at his monologuist best. It has been called 'not a play, but a volume which contains a play'. The third act alone, the so-called 'Don Juan in Hell' scene, is frequently extracted and performed on its own. John Tanner, a morally passionate rationalist, a liberal who steadfastly resents all traditions (like Shaw himself), is pursued and conquered by Anne Whitefield, an overwhelmingly charming and witty creature whose guardian he has become.

John Tanner is described as follows by Shaw: 'He is too young to be described simply as a big man with a beard. But it is already plain that middle life will find him in that category. He has still some of the slimness of youth; but youthfulness is not the effect he aims at; his frock coat would befit a prime minister; and a certain high-chested carriage of the shoulder; a lofty pose of the head and the Olympian majesty with which a mane, or rather a huge wisp, of hazel-coloured hair is thrown back from an imposing brow, suggest Jupiter rather than Apollo. He is prodigiously fluent of speech, restless, excitable (mark the snorting nostril and the restless blue eye, just the thirty-secondth of an inch too wide open), possibly a little mad. He is carefully dressed, not from the vanity that cannot resist finery, but from a sense of the importance of everything he does which leads him to make as much of paying a call as other men do of getting married or laying a foundation stone. A sensitive, susceptible, exaggerative, earnest man: a megalomaniac, who would be lost without a sense of humour.' This last piece of information is extremely important for the actor. If Tanner appears too dry, didactic and rhetorical both the speech and the charm of the man evaporate into a blur of words. All of the images must be personalised and particularised. Tanner is debating with himself and the speech is highly structured and balanced between two contending positions. Mark your breathing and spread your voice throughout the speech so that there is an apparent ease over the long haul. Within the long sentences isolate the separate clauses, rather than individual words, to encapsulate the main ideas and their opposites. That is the essence of Shavian acting. Work confidently using each of the complete sentences as you construct a finely paced argument. You want to arrive at the conclusion of a sentence with the thought clearly expressed and at the end of a speech with a myriad of thoughts contending with one another in a play of ideas.

The Playboy of the Western World
(1907) J M Synge

Act 2. Ireland. The interior of a country public house or shebeen, very rough and untidy, in a village on a wild coast of Mayo. A brilliant morning.

Christopher (Christy) Mahon (20s), 'a slight young man', 'looking bright and cheerful, is cleaning a girl's boots'. Recently arrived, he has been taken in by Michael James Flaherty, a local publican, and is feeling very at home in his new surroundings which he surveys with pride and wonder. He opens the second act with this monologue.

CHRISTY (*to himself, counting jugs on dresser*).
Half a hundred beyond. Ten there. A score that's above. Eighty jugs. Six cups and a broken one. Two plates. A power of glasses. Bottles, a schoolmaster'd be hard set to count, and enough in them, I'm thinking, to drunken all the wealth and wisdom of the county Clare. (*He puts down the boot carefully.*) There's her boots now, nice and decent for her evening use, and isn't it grand brushes she has? (*He puts them down and goes by degrees to the looking-glass.*) Well, this'd be a fine place to be my whole life talking out with swearing Christians, in place of my old dogs and cat; and I stalking around, smoking my pipe and drinking my fill, and never a day's work but drawing a cork an odd time, or wiping a glass, or rinsing out a shiny tumbler for a decent man. (*He takes the looking-glass from the wall and puts it on the back of a chair; then sits down in front of it and begins washing his face.*) Didn't I know rightly, I was handsome, though it was the divil's own mirror we had beyond, would twist a squint across an angel's brow; and I'll be growing fine from this day, the way I'll have a soft lovely skin on me

and won't be the like of the clumsy young fellows do be ploughing all times in the earth and dung. (*He starts.*) Is she coming again? (*He looks out.*) Stranger girls. God help me, where'll I hide myself away and my long neck naked to the world? (*He looks out.*) I'd best go to the room maybe till I'm dressed again.

COMMENTARY: Synge's *The Playboy of the Western World* is a colloquial Irish comedy set in a small village. It focuses on a recent arrival to the village, Christy Mahon, who the villagers think has killed his father. The tale of his deed has turned him into a local hero. He goes to work in a pub, and Pegeen Mike, the daughter of the publican, vies with the Widow Quinn for the affection of this 'brave' lad. His timidity turns to arrogance as he begins to believe in his own lies. When his father appears (not killed after all), the opinion of the townspeople is reversed and he leaves a disillusioned but wiser young man. The liveliness of the dialogue is what makes this such a celebrated classic comedy.

An untutored and naïve country boy who is intuitively imaginative, Christy surveys his modest domain as though he were cataloguing a house of treasures and with bottles and glasses he creates a world he would love to lord it over. These are far better circumstances to be in than the hovel from which he came. When he first appeared in Act One he was a filthy and frightened creature. Here he appears newborn. He begins to spread his wings and see possibilities for himself. Using the glass he takes stock of his reflection and thinks himself not too bad-looking. The actor has to catch the fact that Christy is transforming from one self-image into another. There is a good deal of wonder in the speech and poetic rhythms are used to carry the actor along. There is a lot of action going on in the scene too: counting, polishing, picking things up, washing, preening, looking out the window and running off-stage. Coordinate these actions with the lines. As soon as he sees people at the window, he panics and deflates back to his original mouse-like self and scurries away to hide.

Heartbreak House
(1919) Bernard Shaw

Act 2. The drawing-room of Captain Shotover's house in the middle of the Sussex countryside.

Boss Mangan in Shaw's own description is 'about fiftyfive, with a careworn, mistrustful expression, standing a little on an entirely imaginary dignity, with a dull complexion, straight, lustreless hair, and features so entirely commonplace that it is impossible to describe them.' He has just come from dinner and is in the company of the young and vivacious Ellie Dunn to whom he is engaged. There is a significant age gap between them. Mangan invested in Ellie's father's business, causing the latter's ruin, and here he uncomfortably justifies his actions to her.

MANGAN.
Of course you dont understand: what do you know about business? You just listen and learn. Your father's business was a new business: and I dont start new businesses: I let other fellows start them. They put all their money and their friends' money into starting them. They wear out their souls and bodies trying to make a success of them. Theyre what you call enthusiasts. But the first dead lift of the thing is too much for them; and they havnt enough financial experience. In a year or so they have either to let the whole show go bust, or sell out to a new lot of fellows for a few deferred ordinary shares: that is, if theyre lucky enough to get anything at all. As likely as not the very same thing happens to the new lot. They put in more money and a couple of years more work; and then perhaps they have to sell out to a third lot. If it's really a big thing the third lot will have to sell out too, and leave their work and their money behind them. And thats where the real business man

comes in: where I come in. But I'm cleverer than some: I dont mind dropping a little money to start the process. I took your father's measure. I saw that he had a sound idea, and that he would work himself silly for it if he got the chance. I saw that he was a child in business, and was dead certain to outrun his expenses and be in too great a hurry to wait for his market. I knew that the surest way to ruin a man who doesnt know how to handle money is to give him some. I explained my idea to some friends in the city, and they found the money; for I take no risks in ideas, even when theyre my own. Your father and the friends that ventured their money with him were no more to me than a heap of squeezed lemons. Youve been wasting your gratitude: my kind heart is all rot. I'm sick of it. When I see your father beaming at me with his moist, grateful eyes, regularly wallowing in gratitude, I sometimes feel I must tell him the truth or burst. What stops me is that I know he wouldnt believe me. He'd think it was my modesty, as you did just now. He'd think anything rather than the truth, which is that he's a blamed fool, and I am a man that knows how to take care of himself. (*He throws himself back into the big chair with large self-approval.*) Now what do you think of me Miss Ellie?

COMMENTARY: Shaw's *Heartbreak House* indicts human stupidity, apathy and greed plus the loss of all purpose as the primary causes of the world's problems. It was Shaw's favourite play and closest to the writing of Anton Chekhov. All of the characters are symbolic of some form of human cupidity. Boss Mangan epitomises the capitalist speculator; he neither manufactures nor produces things himself but feeds off the entrepreneurial talents and dreams of others. Eventually he dies when bombs from a German airship fall into the garden of this English Eden.

Mangan is a dry, cold character. He speaks exactly what he thinks and is bereft of any wit, romance or amusement. Notice how gruff and matter-of-fact his language is. He is very much a city financier who takes no risks and hates emotional conflicts. But he also speaks with remarkable honesty as he gives Ellie a basic lesson in modern economics that is tinged with the Darwinian ethic of the survival of the fittest. His language is very simple and direct and not at all typical of Shaw's more principled and garrulous characters. The actor should be reminded that Shaw intended Mangan to be both unpleasant and patronising, but not a melodramatic villain.

Woyzeck
(1836–7) Georg Büchner

Scene 23. A German town. At the pond. Night.

Woyzeck (30) is a pitiful lower class soldier who is the butt of everyone's jokes and derision. In a crime brought on by passion and confusion, perhaps even madness, he has stabbed to death his common-law wife Marie. He returns to the scene of the crime to retrieve his knife and do something with the body.

WOYZECK (*alone*).
The knife!? Where's the knife? I left it here somewhere. It will give me away! Getting closer. Closer. This is a strange place. Weird. What's that noise? Something moving! No. It's all quiet. Over there. Just there – Marie? Aah, Marie! So quiet. Everything is so quiet. Why are you so pale, Marie? What's that red string 'round your neck? A necklace? Did your sins with him earn you that necklace? You were black with sins, Marie, black. Was it I who made you white again? Why is your hair all tangled, Marie? Didn't you comb and braid it today? What's this here? The knife! The knife! I've got it! I'll get rid of it! (*He runs into the water.*) There! Into the water! (*He throws the knife in.*) It sinks like a stone down into the black water. The moon's like a sword with blood on it. No – it's not out far enough – they swim there! (*He goes deeper into the pond and throws it out further.*) There! That's it! But in the summer when they go diving for mussels –? Ha! It'll be rusty then. Who'd ever notice it? But I should have broken it into pieces. Am I still bloody? I'd best wash up. There's a spot and here's another . . . (*He goes deeper into the water.*)

COMMENTARY: Büchner's *Woyzeck* is a tragedy that was written in 1836, but not published until 1879, nor performed until 1913. The script was left in unordered fragments at the author's death (at the age of twenty-three) and so there is no definitive version of the play. Büchner based the drama on the actual murder case of a barber who stabbed his mistress in a fit of jealousy and was then sentenced to death. The playwright adds to the drama by showing that other psychic forces are at work on Woyzeck (like class, science, environment, atmosphere and religion), leading him to distraction as he commits a crime he does not want to commit. Woyzeck, though a good man, is used and manipulated by everyone in the play. His sense of identity and self whittles away to nothing. The play radically influenced both naturalist and expressionist drama.

The speech, like the play itself, is loaded with fragments and telegraphed thoughts. It is written as a series of impulses as Woyzeck is reduced to being a haunted ghost of a man. Words lead him on: 'knife, knife'; 'closer, closer'. The moonlit night, the eeriness of the water, beckon him back to the scene of the crime. The intensity of the moment sharpens everything so that Woyzeck sees objects in close-up: the knife, the string of blood around Marie's throat that glistens like jewels. Woyzeck is oddly distanced from the horror of the event and the fact of death. He is more concerned about being discovered than about the immorality of the crime. Büchner's great achievement was the creation of a largely unknowable and amoral character. The actor must himself provide the reasons why Woyzeck acts as he does. The play provides no answers. The language is gruff and unremarkable except in the few poetic touches, such as 'The moon's like a sword with blood on it.' Though practically all in black and white the addition of red gives an otherwise monochromatic scene a vivid contrast. A major challenge for the actor is how to produce the outdoor setting, discovering the body, then the knife, wading into the water with it, and then wading deeper as if into a fade-out scene in a film.

The Government Inspector
(1836) Nikolai Gogol

Act 3. A reception room of the Mayor's house in a provincial Russian town.

Ivan Alexandrovich Khlestakov (23), an impoverished junior clerk, has lost all his money at cards and is staying in the local inn of a provincial town. The officials and inhabitants of the town have discovered that an important government inspector will be visiting their town incognito to check up on them and their affairs. In their panic that their corruption and rampant bribery will be discovered, they mistake Khlestakov for the government inspector. Although taken aback at first he decides to take them for a ride by impersonating the anticipated inspector and accepting all their hospitality and bribes. Here in the third act he has grown into the role and gives an impromptu of his fantasy life in St Petersburg.

KHLESTAKOV.
Well, you see I live for literature. My house is the finest in the whole of St Petersburg. It's known to everyone as Ivan Alexandrovich Khlestakov's house. (*Turning to everyone.*) I entreat you dear people, if you're ever in Petersburg, do drop by for a visit. And, of course you do know that I give balls. . . . The like of which it's hard to describe. Now, for example, on the table there will be a watermelon – seven hundred rubles worth of watermelon! A tureen of soup will have arrived by ship direct from Paris, and when the lid is removed – well, the aroma, it's just out of this world! Every day I will go to a ball. Then, of course, we have our foursome for whist – the Minister for Foreign Affairs, the French Ambassador, the German Ambassador and me. You just can't imagine how exhausting it is to play cards! I can tell you I've never experienced anything quite like it. After

each ball I'll dash home, run up the stairs to my room and shout to the cook 'Hey, Mavrushka, grab my coat.' . . . Oh silly me, what am I talking about? Well, of course, it just slipped my mind that I live on the first floor. That staircase of mine alone is worth . . . It would interest you to see who gathers in my vestibule even before I'm up in the morning – there are Counts and Princes all squashed together, rubbing shoulders, buzzing away like bees, *bzzz, bzzz*. Sometimes, too, the Minister . . . (*At this the Mayor and the others rise from their seats in awe.*) Actually, my letters are addressed to 'Your Excellency . . .' Once, I took command of a whole department. Bit of an odd business that was. The director left, but not a soul knew where he'd disappeared to. Well, as I'm sure you can imagine, there were all sorts of rumours – what was to be done? who would take his place? There were Generals queueing up to take that Department, but no sooner were they in the job than they discovered it was just too much for them. Looked like it'd be a piece of cake, but it was a devil of a job. Just when it began looking like a complete catastrophe – they turn to me. Immediately government messengers were despatched, more messengers and then even more messengers were soon thronging the streets . . . Would you believe there were 35,000 messengers in all! What do you think of that? 'Ivan Alexandrovich you must take command of the Department!' they say. I can tell you I was a bit taken aback at that. Well I'd come out in my dressing-gown, and my instinct was to decline, but then I realised this could well reach the ears of the Tsar himself, and there was also my official service record to consider . . . 'Very well, gentlemen, I accept,' I said. 'But . . . there's to be no nonsense now . . . you understand me . . . no . . . er . . . I've got ears you know . . . I . . .' And that's just how it was. Every time I'd walk through that department it was like an earthquake had hit the place, all of them trembling and shaking. (*Khlestakov gets more excited*.) Oh no, you don't mess with me. I let them know what was what. Even the State Council fears me. And so they should. I've that kind of power. I'm that kind of man. I'll tell you what I told them – 'I know what's what.' I go everywhere, everywhere. Oh yes, every day I'm at the palace. And tomorrow they're going to make me a Field Marshal! (*At this he slips and falls flat on his face.*)

COMMENTARY: Gogol's *The Government Inspector* is a classic comedy of mistaken identity. A petty provincial town is thrown into turmoil at the disclosure that a government inspector is coming in disguise to investigate their affairs. They immediately jump to the conclusion that the wimpish, solitary clerk holding up in their local inn must be the official in question. It does not take long before the clerk, Khlestakov, is completely into the role and compounds the town's expectations with fantasies of his own. Eventually he is exposed by the local postmaster and the town waits in renewed terror, hearing that the real Inspector General has arrived.

This is how Gogol described Khlestakov in his notes: he is 'thin and slender, rather stupid, and, so the saying goes, a bit dim. In any government office they'd call him silly. He speaks and moves impulsively. He cannot give anything his concentrated attention. His speech is abrupt and words tumble unexpectedly from his mouth. The more the actor playing this role reveals frankness and simplicity the more he will succeed. He is dressed in the very latest fashions.' This is a bravura monologue. Once started there is no turning back. The speech grows and swells as the character inflates and multiplies his lies. His audience is enthralled by each of his exaggerated details and like any captive audience they must be ooh-ing and ah-ing at Khlestakov's apparently extravagant lifestyle. The actor must get carried away by the improvisatory momentum that he keeps embroidering. A sentence barely ends before a new one is tacked on. The actor must decide how real to make Khlestakov. All of Gogol's characters are gross caricatures but they are also consumed by obsessions and egos that are susceptible to flattery and inflation. Notice the image of the earthquake 'trembling and shaking' which presages his own tumble at the end of the speech.

A Month in the Country
(1850) Ivan Turgenev

Act 2. The garden of a Russian country estate. Summer.

Mikhail Alexandrovitch Rakitin (30) is intelligent but ineffectual. He is infatuated with Natalya Petrovna. She taunts and teases him. Together they amuse themselves in a game of cat and mouse. He likes 'observing people, dissecting them, delving deeply into them'. Here we see him doing just that, but on himself this time.

RAKITIN.
What's the matter with her? (*Pauses.*) A whim. Is that it? I've never seen her like this before. Quite the opposite: I don't know any woman less temperamental than she is. What's causing it? (*Walks up and down, suddenly stops.*) How ridiculous is a man with only a single thought in his head, with one focus, one concern in his life . . . Like me, for instance. What she said was right: if one focuses on trivial things from sunrise to sunset then one's bound to become trivial too . . . That's right. But I can't live without her – just being in her presence makes me feel ecstatic; a feeling that can't be defined in words – I am hers completely. If I had to give her up . . . and I'm not exaggerating – I'd give up on life itself. What's the matter with her? Why is she so skittish? What did her sarcastic words mean? Is she getting tired of me? Hmm. (*Sits.*) I've never deceived myself, I know exactly how she loves me; but I did hope that her restrained feelings . . . I *did* hope? Do I have the right to hope, can I dare to hope? I admit my position is quite ridiculous . . . almost contemptible . . . (*Pauses.*) What's the point of talking like that? She's an honest woman and I'm no Casanova (*With a bitter smile.*) – sad to

say. (*Gets up.*) Right . . . that's quite enough of that nonsense. (*Walks up and down.*) What a marvellous day! (*Pauses.*) How expertly she stung me! . . . My 'exquisitely wrought phrases' . . . She's very quick-witted, particularly when she's in a bad mood. And why this sudden enthusiasm for youth and innocence? . . . This tutor . . . she often mentions him. I can't say that I see anything particularly remarkable about him, he's just like any other student. Oh she can't – oh no that's not possible. She's just in a bad mood . . . doesn't know what she wants and so she lashes out at me, like a child hitting its nurse . . . what a flattering comparison! It's as well to let her go her own way. Once all this moodiness is over, she'll be the first to laugh at this skinny boy, this immature youth . . . That's not a bad explanation Mikhail Alexandrovitch, but is it true? God only knows. Well, we'll see. It's not the first time, old boy, that you've had to abandon all your wild ideas and theories, calmly folding your hands and meekly waiting to see what the upshot was. And in the meantime, you have to confess that you feel bitter and pretty stupid . . . But then, that's the way I am, so it seems . . .

COMMENTARY: Turgenev's *A Month in the Country* is a bitter-sweet comedy which focuses on the romantic entanglements that disrupt the routine harmony of life on a country estate. Natalya Petrovna, the wife of the estate owner Islayev, falls in love with her son's young tutor. The affair is complicated by the fact that she thinks she has a rival in Vera, her seventeen-year-old stepdaughter. A family friend, Rakitin, a frequent visitor to the estate, is in love with Natalya, adding another level of complication and rivalry. All of this is brought to a climax when the tutor reveals that he too loves Natalya. The play ends with everyone left heartbroken but wiser.

Rakitin is confused by the sudden behaviour of Natalya. In his speech he tries to sort out the signals she is sending him. The speech does not move the plot along, but stops the action so that the character can take the time to ponder events and his reaction to them. Turgenev's method is to allow a character time for psychological exploration of emotions and motivations. Notice the pauses and the different stances Rakitin takes: he walks, he sits, he abruptly rises, he turns about, his physical state duplicates the restless confusion of his thoughts. He is constantly caught up in an either/or debate with himself. It is typical of the character to vacillate with civilised grace. He is neither angry nor in despair. He is neither direct nor confident. He loves Natalya but mainly from afar, and will do nothing to disrupt the domestic bliss which he, along with everyone else, works very hard to maintain. His last line is a key to his open-ended indecision: 'But then, that's the way I am, so it seems . . .'

A Doll's House
(1879) Henrik Ibsen

Act 3. Norway. A room furnished not expensively but comfortably and tastefully. It is evening.

Torvald Helmer (30s–40s) is a successful lawyer and bank manager. He has been married to his wife Nora for eight years and has kept her pampered, protected and isolated at home. He treats her like a child, giving her the nickname 'Little Squirrel'. However, Nora, having forged a signature on a cheque to get the money to pay for a life-saving holiday for her husband, is now being threatened with blackmail by the moneylender Nils Krogstad. This evening the couple have been to a party where Helmer consumed a lot of champagne. After coming home Helmer opens a letter from Krogstad threatening that the only way to avoid a scandal is if Helmer creates a position for Krogstad at the bank. Helmer confronts Nora with the contents of this letter.

HELMER.
Enough of your play-acting! (*Locking the door.*) Now you're going to stay right here and give me a full explanation. Do you understand what you've done? Answer me! Do you understand! . . . (*Striding about.*) What an eye-opener! During those eight years – she who was my pride and joy – a hypocrite and liar – worse, yes worse – a criminal! Oh it's so disgusting! The disgrace, the shame! (*Nora says nothing and continues to stare straight at him. He stops in front of her.*) I should've guessed something like this would happen. I should've known. What with your father and those foolish, misguided ways of his – Listen to me! – I'll repeat myself – your father and all his foolish, misguided ways have been passed on directly to you! No religion, no morals, no sense of duty! Oh and how I'm punished for turning a blind eye to his stupidity. But I did it for your sake and now you go

and reward me with this . . . Now you've ruined all my happiness. You've just destroyed my whole future. Oh it's too awful to even think about it. I'm entirely at the mercy of that mean little bastard; he can do whatever he pleases with me, get what he wants, order me about – and yet I can't do a thing about him. I'm going to be miserably humiliated and all thanks to this flighty, feeble woman . . . If he were to make all of this public, which he might well do, it could easily look as if I were an accomplice to your crime. People might even think that I was the one behind it all – the one who put you up to it. It's you I should thank for all of this, you who I supported so protectively through all those years of marriage! Is it becoming clear just what you've done to me? . . . It's so incredible I just can't believe it. We've got to find some way out. Take off that shawl. Take it off, I said! Somehow I've got to buy him off. It doesn't matter what it costs; this has to be hushed up. In terms of our relationship – to the outside world, everything must appear just as before. Mind you, only *appear*, of course. Therefore you will continue to live in this house. That's understood. However I'll have the children taken away from your control. I can't risk trusting you with them any longer. Oh, having to say all this to the woman I once loved so much – and who I still –! No, all that has got to end. From now on happiness won't enter into it; we must just endeavour to save what scraps and shreds . . .

The front door bell rings. Helmer starts.

Who can that be? At this time of night? It couldn't be –? He wouldn't –? Hide yourself Nora. . . .

Nora does not move. Helmer goes to open the door.

COMMENTARY: Ibsen's *A Doll's House* uses elements of the problem play with intrigue and some melodrama to probe a marriage that is based on false premises. The image of a wife trapped in a marriage has had a resonant influence down through the decades. Nora's selfless act to aid her husband is greeted by his harsh and unremitting anger. On the basis of that reaction, Nora leaves Helmer and her children, with the famous slamming of the door, to seek some kind of life in which she can be more than his plaything.

Torvald Helmer's unremitting castigation of his wife reveals a temper untouched by love or sympathy. At last the tyrant surfaces in the man. Notice how he reveals his deeper resentments towards Nora and her father. To be perfectly fair though, the actor must see that to Helmer, financial chicanery is a mortal sin. He is a banker and expects his house to be run like a bank as well. He seems to see Nora as either a fragile doll or a criminal; there is no middle ground. Throughout the play we have seen examples of her flightiness so some of Helmer's aggravation has a genuine source. Appearances, however, are everything and social disgrace is his worst fear. All evening he has been drinking champagne so you can imagine that the alcohol releases both his tongue and the venomous anger. Notice how physical he has become in his rage: locking the door, striding about. It is as if he is trying to rein in a violent tendency. He threatens Nora with both his words and his physical presence. Here he shows himself to be a completely different kind of man than the one seen elsewhere in the play.

Miss Julie
(1888) August Strindberg

A large kitchen in a Swedish country house. Midsummer eve.

Jean (30) is a valet in the house of Miss Julie's father, the Count. He is engaged to Kristin, the cook. Jean is confident and intelligent and ambitiously dreams of moving up in the world. Miss Julie is the incarnation of all he aspires to. Miss Julie enjoys mixing with the servants on her father's estate and during the Midsummer celebrations she visits the kitchen. She and Jean engage in seductive, provocative chat. At one point Jean boldly kisses Miss Julie and she retaliates by boxing his ears. But, as in a game of cat and mouse, they resume their taunting conversation. Here he recounts how as a child he became infatuated with her.

JEAN.
It's easy to say that now. But you despise me just the same. . . . Anyway – one day I entered that Garden of Paradise with my mother, to weed the onion beds. Right by the vegetable garden was a Turkish pavilion, shaded by jasmine and overgrown with honeysuckle. I'd no idea what it was used for, but I'd never seen such a beautiful building. People would go inside, and then come out again. And one day, the door was left open. I sneaked in and saw the walls covered with pictures of emperors and kings, and at the windows there were red curtains with tassels hanging down – You do know the place I'm talking about – don't you? . . . I . . . (*He snaps off a piece of lilac and holds it under Miss Julie's nose.*) I'd never been inside the big house – only ever been inside a church. But this was much more beautiful. It didn't matter what I tried to think about, my thoughts would always return to that place. A desire kept growing in me to experience completely the delights of that

place . . . *Enfin*. I crept in, took it all in, and marvelled. Then I heard someone coming! For the upper classes there was only the one exit. But for me, there was another. Since I had no choice, I took it. . . . (*Julie, having accepted the lilac offered by Jean, lets it drop onto the table*.) Then I bolted, plunging through raspberry bushes, scrambling across strawberry beds, ending up on the rose terrace. There I spotted a pink dress and a pair of white stockings – That was you. I scrambled under a pile of weeds and hid there – just imagine lying under that stinking, soggy earth with all those thistles pricking me. I watched you walk among your roses. I said to myself 'If it's true that a thief can enter heaven and be with the angels, then why can't a poor man's child, here on God's earth, enter the Count's garden and play with his daughter.' . . . So, do you know what I did next? I leapt into the millstream, with all my clothes on. Got fished out, and was given a good beating. But next Sunday, when father and all the family had gone to my grandmother's I made sure I was left at home. I washed myself thoroughly with warm water and soap, put on my best clothes and went to church. I knew I'd see you there. I saw you . . . I went back home determined to die. But I wanted a death that was comfortable and peaceful – free of all pain. Suddenly I remembered that it was supposed to be dangerous to sleep under an elder bush. We had a big one in full bloom. So I ripped off every one of those flowers and created a bed for myself in the oat-bin. Have you ever noticed how silky and smooth oats are? Soft as human skin . . . Then I pulled the lid tight, shut my eyes and fell into a deep sleep. When they found me and woke me up I was really, really sick. But, as you see, I didn't die. I don't know what I was trying to prove. I had no hope of gaining you – but you were a symbol, warning me of the absolute futility of ever trying to escape from the class of my birth.

COMMENTARY: Strindberg's *Miss Julie* is a long one-act tragedy which charts the rise and fall of a one-night relationship between the aristocratic Miss Julie and her father's ambitious valet Jean. Their initial seduction and lovemaking eventually turn to quarrels and a brutal falling-out. The play culminates with Miss Julie leaving the stage to commit suicide and Jean left on-stage to face the returning Count, Julie's father. Two opposing poles are used to frame the action: upper versus lower class, night versus day, love versus hate, affection versus lust, mistress versus servant, and man versus woman. In Strindberg's world the conflict between the sexes is the most critical one of all and he pits two formidable antagonists against each other.

Jean's speech is more like a dream fantasy than a memory of how events actually happened. The actor must decide for himself how genuine Jean is being here or how much he is just making it up. The speech is cleverly structured as a rising and falling action to mirror Jean's high-class aspirations and low-class circumstances. The compelling image at the centre of the speech is an outdoor toilet disguised to look like an exotic pavilion (you must make of that symbolism what you will). His speech is also a *tour-de-force* of imaginative writing. It reads like a chase scene in a screenplay. At various points the actor has to speed up and slow down his rhythms. The speech also exposes Jean's impulsiveness, curiosity and desperate desire to improve his lot. Images pass by in isolation, i.e. 'a pink dress and a pair of white stockings'. The writer has done away with lots of connecting bits in order to hurl the action onwards and put you right in the centre of the events. Think of the speech as a string of sense memories that rush by like slides on a screen: sight, hearing, touch, pain, delight, anger. All are filtered through Jean's fragmented story.

The Seagull
(1896) Anton Chekhov

Act 1. A section of a park on a Russian estate before an improvised stage. Summer evening.

Konstantin (25) is the son of a famous but ageing Moscow actress, Arkadina. He lives on his uncle's estate, struggling to become a writer. He has written a play which will be performed before his mother and invited guests that evening. While he waits impatiently for Nina, the young local girl from across the lake who is his leading actress, he confides in his uncle Sorin. He reveals that he has an impossible relationship with his mother, who is having an affair with a famous novelist. The fame of both of them seems to deny Konstantin an identity of his own.

KONSTANTIN (*tearing the petals of a flower*).
She loves me – she loves me not . . . She loves me – she loves me not . . . She loves me – she loves me not. (*Laughing.*) You see, my mother doesn't love me. Of course she doesn't. What she wants is to live, love and wear revealing dresses. And here am I, already twenty-five years old, a constant reminder that she's not young any longer. When I'm not around, she's thirty-two – when I am she's forty-three . . . and for that, she hates me. Besides, she knows I don't care for the theatre. She loves the theatre – she thinks she's saving mankind and the sacred cause of art, but in my opinion her precious modern theatre is conservative and narrow-minded. When the curtain rises on an artificially lit room, with its three walls – these artists, these geniuses, these priests of sacred art, show us how people eat, drink, make love, move about and wear their jackets. When they strain to show significance in the utmost banalities, and try to pluck moralities out of humdrum

homilies, to reveal pat little morals for everyday use; when in a thousand different guises they serve up the same tired, turgid things, again and again and again – then I run and keep on running, just like Maupassant fleeing from the sight of the Eiffel Tower, when its blatant vulgarity set his mind reeling. . . . We need new artistic forms, new means of expression. And if we can't have them, then it's better to have none at all. (*Looking at his watch.*) I love my mother – I love her very much. But then, she leads such a ridiculous life, always fussing over that novelist, her name forever cropping up in the papers . . . I'm tired of it all. Sometimes, the sheer egotism of an ordinary mortal makes me regret that my mother is a famous actress, and it seems to me that were she just an ordinary woman, then I should be much happier. Uncle, what could be more hopeless and stupid than my situation? Especially when my mother is surrounded by all her guests, all those celebrities, artists and writers – among them, I'm the only one who's a nobody. Oh they tolerate me, but only because I'm her son. Who am I? What am I? I never graduated from university, due, so the saying goes, to circumstances beyond my control. I've no talents, I've not a penny of my own, and according to my passport, I'm a petty bourgeois from Kiev. My father, you see, even though he was a famous actor, was still an ordinary petty bourgeois from Kiev. So when these artistic friends of hers would happen to notice me in her salon, I could feel their eyes measuring my insignificance – I guessed what they were thinking. It was humiliating.

COMMENTARY: *The Seagull* is partly about the ambitions of a young would-be actress Nina and a burgeoning writer Konstantin, to flee their isolation and loneliness in order to establish themselves as individuals and artists in their own right. Though in love here at the beginning of the action when Konstantin stages his first experimental play and Nina gets a taste of the stage for the first time, circumstances and other characters drive them apart until they are reunited briefly and then part again in the final act. The play concludes with Konstantin's off-stage suicide.

By creating an ingenious series of interlocking triangular relationships and sudden shifts in mood, and by having them talk obsessively about someone else, Chekhov always increases the tensions and frustrations between his characters. Konstantin cannot talk about his problems to his kindly old uncle without erupting into fits of jealous anger about his mother and all she represents. Although we have yet to see her on-stage, Konstantin's extended description gives her a vivid presence which her later entrance only confirms. His fixation on her is pronounced and he is clearly made to feel like an irritating obstruction in her life. What he has done is revolt against everything she admires and stands for. The play he will present tonight is antithetical to the kind of theatre she represents, so it is a calculated subversive act on his part. The symbolism of the play also runs counter to the realistic literature favoured by his mother's lover Trigorin, a successful older writer whom Konstantin detests. Throughout the play Konstantin is given to performing these disruptive scenes: later he attempts suicide and in the end succeeds at it. His dark, brooding mood never leaves him except for brief moments with Nina. She is a kind of alternative and hope, even though she later rejects him for Trigorin. Opening the monologue with the flower, Konstantin childishly proves the hopelessness of his state. Though in his mid-twenties he sounds like a petulant adolescent. In performing the monologue the actor must take into account how Sorin might be reacting to the vociferousness of Konstantin's resentment. Notice, too, that Konstantin uses words extremely well and is given to making acid pronouncements; a good sign that he will become the outsider he most wants to be.

The Dance of Death
(1900) August Strindberg

Part 1. Act 2, scene 2. Sweden. The interior of a circular fortress tower of grey stone furnished as a sitting-room. Evening.

Edgar (50s), the Captain, is the commanding officer of a military fortress on an island off the coast of Sweden. He and his wife Alice (ten years his junior and a former actress) are approaching their twenty-fifth wedding anniversary. Over the years their relationship has deteriorated into an endless round of bitter acrimony and resentful quarrels. They hate rather than love. Every encounter between them is a chance to settle scores in their on-going marital battle. Cut off on the island, 'Little Hell', they are bored and isolated. Alice's cousin Kurt visits them and becomes attracted to Alice. In the meantime, much to Alice's delight, the Captain suffers two heart attacks. Finding this bizarre atmosphere too much to handle Kurt leaves the fortress and this leads the Captain and Alice to an almost comic reconciliation. This speech of the Captain's closes the first part of this play. He wears a worn uniform and riding boots.

THE CAPTAIN.

. . . Everyone who comes in contact with us grows evil and moves on. Kurt was weak and evil is strong. (*Pauses.*) Life has no character these days! In the old days one would fight, but now one just blusters around. I'm quite confident that in three months you and I will be celebrating our silver wedding – Kurt will propose the toast and Gerda and the doctor they'll come too. The Ordnance Officer will give a speech, and the Sergeant-Major will lead the cheering. And if I know the Colonel – he'll invite himself along. (*Alice giggles.*) That makes you laugh, does it? Now you do remember Adolf's silver wedding – and that fellow in the hussars? The bride had to wear her wedding ring on the wrong hand because in a flash of passion the bridegroom

138

had chopped off her wedding-ring finger with the blade of a jewelled pen-knife. (*Alice holds her handkerchief to her mouth to stifle her laughter*.) Are you crying? No, you're laughing, aren't you! Yes, child, that's the way it is for us now – as we laugh, we cry, and as we cry, we laugh. And which one's right? Well, don't expect me to know the answer. The other day in the paper I read about this man who'd been divorced seven times, married seven times and finally, in his ninety-ninth year, he elopes and marries his first wife again. That's what I call love! I can't tell you if life's meant to be a drama or a comedy. When it's meant to be serious elements of farce creep in. When it's funny it's all as calm as can be . . . But just when you decide it might be serious, someone comes and makes a complete fool of you. Like Kurt . . . Do you want a silver wedding celebration? (*Alice is silent*.) Alice, say yes, go on say yes . . . So what if they laugh at us – who cares? We'll laugh with them – or be serious – just as we please . . . So then. Our silver wedding. (*Rises*.) We'll cancel the past and move on! So – Let's move on!

COMMENTARY: Strindberg's *The Dance of Death* is a two-part play that works like a tragicomedy. It shifts abruptly from mood to mood (often within a single speech) and the actor must be prepared to go in whatever direction the author chooses. A character laughs when you expect them to cry. Strindberg conceived the play as a claustrophobic battleground in which his celebrated war between the sexes could be played out in splendid isolation. The role of Edgar has attracted some of the greatest modern actors.

Edgar's speech is full of quirks and rapid shifts. He is taunting and playful simultaneously, both father and husband to his wife. He promises and denies. When you play him you have to capture his ability to reach out and pull back in practically the same motion. Throughout the play he endlessly reminisces but you always get the feeling that Edgar is supplying details and elaborating on events that never took place. As with all of Strindberg's best speeches, a grotesque image will suddenly flash in front of you, i.e. the blade of a jewelled penknife severing a wedding-ring finger. The character lives under the threat of a self-imposed death-wish; he has already had two heart attacks. When you play Edgar, however, you must see that his hunger for life ('Let's move on!') keeps him going. The 'dance' in the play is that critical balance between life and death.

The Cherry Orchard
(1904) Anton Chekhov

Act 3. The drawing-room in Madame Ranyevskaya's country estate. Evening.

Yermolay Lopakhin (40s), a businessman and son of a former serf, has just bought the family estate belonging to Madame Ranyevskaya and her brother Gayev. Throughout the play he has been warning them both to pay attention to their affairs to prevent forfeiting their property. They have failed to do so and Lopakhin has purchased the estate himself at an auction earlier that same day. He enters a party scene, having danced and celebrated on his own, and euphorically addresses the guests.

LOPAKHIN.
I bought it! Just hold on a moment please, ladies and gentlemen . . . If you'd be so kind . . . My head's spinning . . . I can't get a word out . . . (*Laughs.*) So we get to the auction and Derigamov is already there. Your brother only had fifteen thousand rubles, and Derigamov immediately bids thirty thousand over and above the mortgage. As soon as I see that, I jump right in and bid forty. He bids forty-five. I go to fifty-five. He's raising by fives and I'm raising by tens. So that was that – all over. I bid the mortgage plus ninety thousand. So it went to me. The cherry orchard's mine now! Mine! Dear God in heaven the cherry orchard is mine! Go on, tell me I'm drunk – tell me I'm delirious, tell me I'm just imagining it . . . (*Stamps his feet.*) No, don't laugh at me! If my father and grandfather could rise from their graves, and see all that's happening . . . how their Yermolay, beaten, illiterate Yermolay, who ran barefoot in winter . . . how that same Yermolay has bought this estate, the most beautiful place in the whole

world . . . I've bought the estate where my grandfather and father were slaves, where they weren't even allowed into the kitchens. I must be dreaming. It's my imagination . . . It's all inside my head. (*Picks up keys and smiles tenderly*.) She threw down those keys to demonstrate that she's not mistress here any longer . . . (*He jangles keys*.) So never mind. (*The sound of a band tuning up*.) You! Musicians, play, I want to hear you! Everybody gather round, watch Lopakhin take an axe to the cherry orchard! Watch the trees as they fall, each one crashing down! We'll build summer cottages, hundreds of summer cottages, and our children and grandchildren, and great-grandchildren will see a new world right here . . . Music! Let's have some music!

COMMENTARY: Chekhov's *The Cherry Orchard* is the last of his great comic dramas depicting the failure of aspirations among a sampling of different character types from high to low, master to servant. The play is a study of the way in which the Ranyevskaya family refuse to sell the cherry orchard in order to settle the debt on their entire estate. They engage in dreams and fantasies about the past but refuse to face the reality of the present and, more importantly, the future. The cherry orchard is a vivid reminder of their youth, nobility and happiness. They refuse to sell it because that would be courting extinction of their way of life. Lopakhin, a freed serf, and new type of rising man, matches their sentimental impracticality with financial practicality. Finally, through a turn of events the whole estate becomes his and the Ranyevskayas are forced to depart.

Lopakhin is deliriously drunk with delight at having won the prize of a lifetime. If only his ancestors could see him now, a serf who now can live in the master's house. Although a good man, there is also something boorish and uncaring about him. He is loud and boastful, thinking almost solely about money and treating life as just one more transaction. He does not think of the impact that his news is having on all present. He is so delirious that he believes he has entered a dreamworld all his own. The actor must seize the opportunity to be as free and as light-headed as possible here. Pull out all the stops. The fate of the cherry orchard has finally been settled. This is a climactic moment: the future of Russia from this point on begins with people like Lopakhin. No one is more aware of the momentousness of this occasion than Lopakhin himself and that is why he treats it as a celebration. Notice the significance of the keys dropped by Varya, Madame Ranyevskaya's daughter. They symbolise his victory and the actor should endow them with a kind of reverence. Lopakhin really grows in stature in this scene, and experiences enormous release.

Play Sources

The Alchemist by Ben Jonson in *Ben Jonson: Three Comedies* (Penguin)

Arden of Feversham, Anonymous (New Mermaids)

The Changeling by Thomas Middleton & William Rowley in *Three Jacobean Tragedies* (Penguin)

The Cherry Orchard by Anton Chekhov (Methuen)

The Constant Couple by George Farquhar (Methuen)

Coriolanus by William Shakespeare (various editions)

The Country Wife by William Wycherley in *Three Restoration Comedies* (Penguin)

The Critic by Richard Brinsley Sheridan in *Richard Brinsley Sheridan: The School For Scandal & Other Plays* (Penguin)

The Dance of Death by August Strindberg in *Strindberg Plays: Two* (Methuen)

Doctor Faustus by Christopher Marlowe in *Christopher Marlowe: The Complete Plays* (Penguin)

A Doll's House by Henrik Ibsen in *Ibsen Plays: Two* (Methuen)

The Double Dealer by William Congreve in *William Congreve: Comedies* (Penguin)

Edward II by Christopher Marlowe in *Christopher Marlowe: The Complete Plays* (Penguin)

The Government Inspector by Nikolai Gogol in *The Government Inspector* (Methuen)

Hamlet by William Shakespeare (various editions)

Heartbreak House by Bernard Shaw (Penguin)

Henry VI (Part 1) by William Shakespeare (various editions)

Hippolytus by Euripides in *Euripides: Alcestis, Iphigenia in Tauris & Hippolytus* (Penguin)

The Honest Whore (Part 1) by Thomas Dekker in *Dramatic Work: Thomas Dekker* (three volumes) (Cambridge University Press)

An Ideal Husband by Oscar Wilde in *Wilde: The Complete Plays* (Methuen)

Lady Windermere's Fan by Oscar Wilde in *Wilde: The Complete Plays* (Methuen)

Libation Bearers by Aeschylus in *Aeschylus Plays: Two* (Methuen)

Life is a Dream by Pedro Calderón de la Barca in *Calderón Plays: One* (Methuen)

Love for Love by William Congreve in *Three Restoration Comedies* (Penguin)

Man and Superman by Bernard Shaw (Penguin)

The Misanthrope by Molière in *Molière: Five Plays* (Methuen)

The Miser by Molière (Methuen)

Miss Julie by August Strindberg in *Strindberg Plays: One* (Methuen)

A Month in the Country by Ivan Turgenev (Penguin)

Oedipus the King by Sophocles in *Sophocles: The Theban Plays* (Methuen)

Phedra by Jean Racine in *Landmarks of French Classical Drama* (Methuen)

The Playboy of the Western World by J M Synge in *Synge: The Complete Plays* (Methuen)

The Provok'd Wife by Sir John Vanbrugh in *Sir John Vanbrugh: Four Comedies* (Penguin)

The Relapse by Sir John Vanbrugh in *Sir John Vanbrugh: Four Comedies* (Penguin)

The Revenger's Tragedy by Cyril Tourneur (*attrib.*) (Methuen)

The Rivals by Richard Brinsley Sheridan in *Richard Brinsley Sheridan: The School For Scandal & Other Plays* (Penguin)

Romeo and Juliet by William Shakespeare (various editions)

The Rover (Part 1) by Aphra Behn in *Behn: Five Plays* (Methuen)

The Seagull by Anton Chekhov (Methuen)

The Second Mrs Tanqueray by Arthur Wing Pinero in *Pinero: Three Plays* (Methuen)

The Spanish Tragedy by Thomas Kyd in *Elizabethan and Jacobean Tragedies* (New Mermaids)

'Tis Pity She's a Whore by John Ford in *John Ford: Three Plays* (Penguin)

Volpone by Ben Jonson in *Ben Jonson: Three Comedies* (Penguin)

The Way of the World by William Congreve in *Four English Comedies* (Penguin)

The White Devil by John Webster in *John Webster: Three Plays* (Penguin)

A Woman Killed with Kindness by Thomas Heywood (New Mermaids)

A Woman of No Importance by Oscar Wilde in *Wilde: The Complete Plays* (Methuen)

Woyzeck by Georg Büchner in *Büchner: The Complete Plays* (Methuen)